SPANNER IN

WORKS

The Prologue

Ian Dury once said, "Good evening, I'm from Essex."

Well, to paraphrase. Good evening, I'm from Middlesex. I know, it doesn't quite have the same ring about it does it - but it is true. Or is it? Apparently, Middlesex doesn't exist anymore. It was abolished in 1965, two years before I was even born, eaten up by Greater London, as the suburbs became part of London. The bit I'm in is technically Surrey.

Good evening, I'm from Surrey. Oh, for fuck's sake. That sounds even worse.

This is kind of my point. You think you're being truthful, but facts get manipulated, memory conveniently files things into some kind of order, even though some of these may be misremembered. Who knows what goes on up there? Most of these stories or anecdotes have been retold over the years, by myself or sometimes others, so it's an approximation. In my mind, these things definitely happened as written here.

I've thought about writing a book on and off, for quite a few years. The premise for writing it, was to jot down a lot of anecdotes relating to funny experiences that happened down my local pub - The Royal Hart in Ashford. Not the one in Kent. The one in Middlesex or Surrey or whatever. Bloody hell, I'm not going over that lot again. It has gone on to be much more than that. I also mention my difficult school years, my gig going, holidays, and life as a Gary Numan obsessive, in the early days at least. I grew up in the same location as the man himself, albeit 10 years later. As a big music fan, I would describe this book as a compilation of my greatest hits. There are a lot of funny stories to do with The Royal Hart, and that is what got me started writing this book in the first place. I'm sure that 50 other old regulars could write about that place, and the anecdotes would be completely different. I started a Facebook group many years ago for yearly reunions, and thought I'd put a shout out on there to see if anyone could help me out with some old recollections. I got about half a dozen replies and I didn't remember any of them, so make of that what you will. I'd love someone else to do a similar thing to this, who used to drink down there from the mid-80s to the turn of the century. These are just my memories mainly.

It really was a fantastic pub. There were some brilliant characters down there who were regulars back in the day, and we had a great time most of the time.

I've been racking my brain to try and remember things that happened from my early days of drinking and going out, but I know I've forgotten 10 times as much as I've remembered. Maybe some of them will come to me as I'm writing this. Edit. Yes, they did!

Before I start, I don't want to embarrass anyone or say anything defamatory against them. In order to bypass this possibility, I will mainly be using first names only. We all did and said silly things back in the day. I didn't get the nickname "Spanner" for nothing, so if you are reading this and you are upset because I have made you look foolish, firstly, I don't think I have, and secondly, that isn't my intention.

Speaking of which, a lot of people ask me how I got the nickname Spanner in the first place.

I'm giving you the answer from my point of view, but you'll have to ask my old mate Ade, as he came up with it. Later on in the book, I mention moving out and renting a house for a year with a couple of mates, Jon and Ade. We were a few years older than your average student, but behaved like them. Drinking and getting up to all sorts of mischief. In fact, I'm pretty sure I got the name before we moved out, but it definitely stuck once we were there. There used to be a Sunday morning tv show which was aimed at late teens like ourselves, who were getting over the revelry from the night before. It was set up by Janet Street-Porter and amongst others, and had Magenta Devine presenting. It featured Max Headroom if you remember him? A Canadian guy who was part animation and part live action. He also had a number 12 hit in 1986 in the UK with

Paranoimia featuring The Art Of Noise. Or maybe the other way around, but I digress. I do a lot of that.

The magazine format of the show featured a 6-minute Gerry Anderson Claymation every week called Dick Spanner, Private Investigator. It was set in America in the future and he was a robotic private investigator. It was done in a film noire style full of intentionally bad puns, but funny. He was incompetent, a bit like Inspecter Clouseau from The Pink Panther, who despite his buffoonery and bumbling about, always seemed to crack the case, more by luck than judgement.

Amongst the 3 of us in the rented house, if we did something stupid, which was pretty frequently, we'd call each other a dick or a spanner. I guess I just did more dicking and spannering about than anyone else, and the name just stuck. Eventually, everyone called me Spanner. Many do to this day. I don't mind it. Anyone can call me it except my wife, Lisa. That I don't like for some reason. It's only the interesting people who get a nickname isn't it?

If you were a regular down the Hart and are not featured in the book, please don't be put out. I've forgotten more than I can remember, and each and every one, made it the place that it was. Even Alfie!

As I say, "Spanner In The Works" is mostly tales of anecdotes from a great pub in Ashford called The Royal Hart. Sadly, it is now an abandoned antiques shop – how appropriate.

Childhood To Teen Spirit

Before I get to the good stuff, I guess I should give you a brief outline of myself.

I was born in a little hospital a few hundred yards away from Hampton Court Palace.

I have an older brother, Clive, and both of my parents died within 4 months of each other in 2022. They both had good lives. My dad went first aged 91 followed by my mum who was 88. I look like my mum but have my dad's sense of humour, albeit a bit lewder than his was. I guess it's a generational thing. I used to go around the corner to see them most Saturdays.

I first met Lisa at the end of 1988 and we finally married on August 12th 1995. Three years later, our only child, Amber was born. We both wanted a girl and we couldn't have been happier when she popped out so we stopped there.

My grandparents on my dad's side and my parents, both ran little, old fashioned (even then) boutique style ladies fashions shops. Both of these were in Ashford when I was born on May 5th 1967. I know, surely that's a mistake – sadly not.

Whilst it wasn't an empire, it did enable me and my brother to grow up in a very nice 4 bedroomed detached property in Ashford. It also meant that we could just about afford to go to local private schools, although money was always tight because of this. I've always found this quite embarrassing and I don't normally mention it to people as they tend to get the wrong impression about private schools – or the ones I went to anyway.

They were nothing like Charterhouse or Eton or somewhere. These were a small step up from comprehensives with ideas of grandeur. I doubt there was very much difference at all except that you had to pay. Maybe the class sizes were slightly smaller, I guess. We still had about 30 per class.

The first was Staines Prep (aged roughly 5 to 10) which I loved every second of. Well, almost. There was one vile teacher. I think she was called Mrs Payne. One day, we were in the classroom - between 20 to 30 of us boys and girls aged about 5 or 6, when she started moaning because there was a horrible farty smell in the classroom. She asked all of us "Who has poo'd their pants?"

Nobody answered. She asked again and again but still no answer.

"Right" she said.

"If you don't admit to it, you are all coming up here one by one and I'm going to pull down your pants!"

I remember thinking it was quite funny at the time. Until it was my turn that is. At this point, I bet you are all thinking that it's me with the stinky pants, aren't you?!!!!!! Well think again. After all of us had been humiliated and after checking everywhere more thoroughly, she realised that none of us had shat ourselves after all. The smell was coming from a rotten chicken carcass, that someone had brought in before the Christmas holidays. We were all asked to bring something in to eat, leading up to the end of term Christmas festivities. I brought in penguin bars- a good choice, I think. She probably put the chicken aside to save for herself and forgot about it. By the time we came back in January, it did bloody well stink. No apology or anything though. She really was a vile woman who threw the kids about like rag dolls at times.

Mostly though, I have good memories of Staines Prep, and although I was never naturally academic, I was liked by most of the teachers and gained a small but loyal gathering of friends.

There was a Canadian teacher called Mr Monger. He was one of those teachers that you just couldn't read. He would probably be diagnosed as bi-polar nowadays. I remember once, I wasn't paying attention in class and he shouted out at the top of his voice (through his intimidating "walrus" moustache)

"SLIFKIN, GET OUTSIDE NOW AND WAIT FOR ME!"

I used to get that sickening, sinking feeling where your whole tummy seemed to churn over inside. By the time he came out with a big stick in his hand I was almost shaking.

"Right" he said, having calmed down completely as he liked me really.

Then, whilst smiling through that tash, he said "I'm going to whack this stick on the table and you have to shout out as loud as you can, then walk back in pretending that you've been caned. Really lay it on thick" he added.

As hard to believe as it is, I was quite a shy kid. I found the idea completely embarrassing and I refused to do it.

"Go on" he whispered.

"It'll scare the hell out of them."

There was no way I was going to do it although I kind of wish I did, but I was really scared still. I think he could see that I was trying to psyche myself up to do it, but it was like trying to pee when someone is watching. It just ain't gonna happen. In the end, I just went back in to the classroom. Everyone stared at me. I could tell that they were thinking that they were glad it was me and not them. I then had to try and pay attention to Vikings or Normans or whatever the hell he was going on about afterwards. His plan worked though – the whole class were now paying close attention. He was ok though really. A real old school character.

There was another teacher who only stayed for a couple of years. He was called Mr Beckham. He did a few academic lessons, but I mainly remember him from games. He could've been mistaken for John Lennon. Long hair and those round spectacles just like the former Beatle. He would voluntarily coach and train with us after school, playing football.

I enjoyed football in games, but my real skill was playing with a tennis ball in break time. We played 3 a side and got really good with controlling the little ball. I could do tricks and keepy uppy for ages. My speciality was doing some tricks, finishing off with volleying the tennis ball, putting swerve on it to go in off the post. The post was a little wooden shelter in the playground. Teachers couldn't believe it as I could do it pretty consistently. Unfortunately, my skills didn't transfer to a normal sized football.

Mr Beckham did all he could and it was great fun. He was partly responsible for my love of football to this day. We found out that he was seeing another teacher. The gorgeous Miss Dear. Even at only 9 or10 years old, I knew she was a catch and I thought good luck to him. In fact, good luck to both of them. A lot of the other kids took the piss out of them in a really immature way like kids do. Pretending to kiss and all that stuff. I stood up for them in the corridor once, telling the other kids that they were out of order, and couldn't they see that they were upsetting them? I hadn't realised that Mr Beckham was right behind and heard me. I was embarrassed (as usual) but he thanked me. I felt very grown up. It's a shame they left soon after. As a footnote, they both drove past me in Ashford high street a few months later, tooting and waving wildly as they drove by. It was nice to be liked.

I had two really good mates. Robbie and Kevin. Robbie and I would always be playing football and singing pop songs.

One day, I remember him saying something like "We should follow music that's in the charts."

I didn't even really know what the charts were and had only seen Top Of The Pops in passing. That's how I can pinpoint my real love for music. I was 10 in 1977. It was the same time as when you could collect little packs of punk rock cards which had bubble gum inside. I have since found out through the wonders of the internet, that they were made by a company called Monty Gum. A lot of them weren't punk, but most of them were. This was my first recollection of knowing what punk was. That and seeing punks in the street with dyed spiky hair and dayglo socks. All thanks to Robbie. I'm sure I would've got there eventually but still; I do remember that. We used to record the charts from the radio on Sunday evenings, and even write them out on paper for a little while. I soon got bored of that though. I started saving up and buying records. Singles mainly plus the occasional album. I won't pretend that I just loved punk. I bought loads of other records. Abba, Darts, Showaddywaddy and plenty of others. I didn't care what was cool, I'd just buy what I heard and liked. I loved owning records though right from the off. My love of collecting vinyl coincided with the popularity of picture covers, coloured vinyl, picture discs and lyric sheets for albums, so it was good timing. You just had to listen to the top 40 on Sunday afternoons, often taping them and trying to cut out the DJ's voice. Eventually I discovered John Peel from 10pm to midnight on weekdays too. That was a whole new avenue of aural pleasure, although he also played a lot of crap too which nobody seems to mention these days.

It was also around this time that when visiting my grandparents every Sunday, my cousin Tony, who is a couple of years older than me, started to bring his vinyl collection to play on the radiogram. That dates us – radiogram!

I remember him having loads of punk and post punk (as it

became known) singles and a few albums. The likes of Generation X, The Jam, XTC. All the good stuff. I just loved it all straight away. Not just the music but the packaging. It was so cool. We went around to his house one day and in his bedroom, he'd taken out all of his 7" vinyl records, put them in to new sleeves, and tacked all of the picture cover sleeves on to his wall. Early Ultravox, The Sex Pistols, 999 etc. It was Tony who had the Down In The Park 12" and Are 'Friends' Electric? picture disc when they came out. I got into collecting soon after and have managed to keep most of my records.

Saturdays were spent kicking a ball about with my brother and Mark from next door. Headers and volleys, rush goalie, jumpers for goalposts. All that bollocks, but I loved it. Well, except when the ball went under an oily parked car and you used to have to get right underneath to drag it out. Sometimes we would go to the park which wasn't far away. You could end up with 30 against 30 over there at the end of the afternoon. "Next goal wins!" We would play board games and stuff too. Later on, his parents bought a pool table which was great for Saturday afternoons. The three of us would play pool with the house to ourselves, as both of his parents worked on Saturdays. I clearly remember hearing Something Better Change by The Stranglers for the first time there whilst playing pool, giggling to the line "Stick my fingers right up your nose!" A happy and privileged childhood. Summers that went on forever, playing around each other's houses. Sneaking into the cinema. All that stuff. Planet Of The Apes properly freaked me out. "They were on Earth all along!" Jaws gave me nightmares. My childhood seemed to go on forever which I'm really thankful for. Haunted House and Jubbly ice lollies, black jack and fruit salad sweets (that was one of our "five a day" back then!)

One thing happened that was not so great though. It was summer time. As a child, it was always summer time somehow. I was playing French cricket with my brother and cousin, Tony, in the park, or rec as we sometimes called it, when out of nowhere, what seemed like a hundred (although it was probably more like 30 to 50) skinheads rampaged over the fence yanking out the wooden blocks from the wire mesh and randomly battering innocents. It really was mindless violence from 20 somethings who came in from Stanwell. Stanwell in those days was a no-go zone. It had a really bad reputation. They battered their way through the park shouting "We're gonna kill you Ashford wankers!" I remember one poor bloke ended up with a broken leg, others were left bleeding. It really was shocking, especially for a shy, 10-year-old kid like myself. We just froze and luckily, they left us alone as they rampaged on in a frenzy. Looking back, I think it's why I still hate confrontation and violence to this day. It also put me off going to football matches until I was about 30 as it seemed that that was the norm at matches in the 70s and 80s, from what I'd read and heard anyway.

I never went to Stanwell until I had to through my job as a courier well into the 90s. I was still very wary. I'm pleased to say that although it's not exactly Monaco, it's no different to any other suburban little village these days. Despite that one off incident, my childhood was pretty much perfect. I wouldn't change a thing.

I should however warn you that it all went a bit "tits up" when I went to big school. Halliford School for boys in Shepperton. Don't worry, it does lighten up once I get passed school but I guess I should put this in here.

Punk had started, hormones had started and I ended up in this shithole with a headmaster who would've made any Sergeant Major in the British army, seem like Mahatma Gandi. We knew him as "Boris" although I don't know why. His real name was Mr Riley and he was an arsehole.

Seriously, I've never met anyone since who was as nasty, unforgiving, dour and evil as that man. That coupled with a few students who took great delight in smashing my (and a few others) faces in on a daily basis, meant it wasn't a great time. I lost all motivation for learning and became troublesome and insecure, which meant I had few friends. The teachers weren't keen on me either. I knew it was going to be tough when on the very first day, the class swat at Staines Prep also moved to this school. As Boris was going through the rules, this kid looked the other way for a second. The bully of a headmaster walked over, shouted at him why he wasn't paying attention. He wasn't able to answer, so he got a really hard slap on the head. He was left crying and shaking with fear. He was 11 years old. This was the best-behaved kid amongst us. What the fuck were we gonna do? Welcome to the next 5 years!

I was a late developer I think it is fair to say, physically and mentally and I had little interest in academia. I got bored easily, didn't do my homework and just got into trouble for lots of small things. I was never a bad kid though.

I received the cane on 3 different occasions for what I consider to be fairly mild, insubordinate behaviour, like scribbling on a text book or not paying attention. For the third time, I knew it was coming. My teacher told me to do 100 lines for not doing my homework. I didn't do it so he doubled it. I still didn't do it so he told me that I'd have to hand it in tomorrow with my homework. As punishment, it had now become 500 lines. Not even Keith Richards has done that many. I was an idiot. I started to do it but it was just too many. I had Mr Andrews for last lesson. He went over the lines and said I hadn't finished. I said it was too many and I was getting cramp in my hand. He then told me that I'd have to see the head in the morning. I knew I was going to get the cane so I did that old trick. I went to school with about 5 exercise books down my pants.

I'll take 6 of the best, at least I won't have to spend all evening doing those bloody lines I thought. My prediction was correct. He must've seen the books down there but he didn't say anything. I pretended to yelp after each blow. I was scared, but it didn't hurt at all. Result. Well, it was, until he told me that I'd still have to hand the rest of the lines in by the morning. I couldn't believe it. I did somehow manage it. Why didn't I just do that in the first place?

I was an idiot and didn't help myself.

It also didn't help that my best mate Nicky got expelled. He was a bit of a nutter and was well into punk. He had a rich dad and got all the gear from the King's Road. Bondage trousers with bum flaps, leather jackets, ripped t-shirts, all that stuff. He'd sometimes bring his gear into school. He once rang me up at home and asked me to go up town with him, but my mum found out and wouldn't let me go. Tragic. The thing about Nicky was, he could look after himself. Even kids bigger and older than him stood no chance because he went all in. It seems ridiculous as we were only 12 or 13. He was a good mate to have though. If he caught anyone having a go at me, he'd kick the shit out of them. No questions asked. However, when he got expelled for drug taking, it left me even more vulnerable.

In the summer holidays, one of the older kids managed to sneak in to the school and graffiti pretty much everywhere. It was epic. We were all called in to a special assembly in the main hall. There was Mr Riley on the stage full of fury and adamant that the culprit would be caught. Behind him, sprayed on to the back wall in massive letters read "BORIS IS A FUCKING WANKER."

He was right though. He did get caught as the dozy twat left the spray cans in his desk. He was a 5th former who naturally denied it. Mr Andrews, the teacher who gave me all the lines, used to be a copper though and was able to prove it was him from his fingerprints. He got expelled. Worth it though.

The following year, this new kid arrived. His second name was Winterbaum. I genuinely thought it was Winterbum and it seemed really funny to me. I called him it a few times over the next couple of days. He was built like a shit brickhouse (yes, I know that's the wrong way round but it amuses me).

He soon became ringleader of a little gang. They probably thought it better to join than be on the other end. I don't blame them really.

He was a typical bully. Taking the piss, belittling and removing all of my self-confidence, what there was of it. Once he'd done that, he just used plain violence against me. Pretty much every day for the next 3 years of schooling, I'd be either trying to avoid him, or getting beaten up by him and his cronies. He wasn't the only one either as I'd become an easy target by then. I never fought back. That shit only happens in films. If I did, he would've retaliated even harder. He was a big strong lump.

When I hear the music for Mastermind on television, I still get nervous to this day, knowing that I'm back into school in the morning for more beatings and getting into trouble for not doing my homework.

I was not in a good place. I did as little work as I could get away with, had a bad attitude and was getting battered and bruised daily. Not a good combination. I didn't tell anyone until I met Lisa many years later. That was a lot of shit to bottle up for all those years. It must've affected me at the time.

It seemed like I was in for a surprise. Not a good one either.

In the summer holidays, my dad told me that we're going out, so I got in the car with him. I kept asking him where we were going but he remained tight lipped.

I wondered why we were heading in the direction of the school but hoped it was a coincidence. I couldn't believe it when we pulled into the school carpark. The next thing I knew was that we were heading for the headmaster's office. We were summoned in. The headmaster started chatting about my conduct, but he behaved completely differently in front of my dad. It was obvious however, that he wanted me out. Probably because he knew I wouldn't be good for his school exam stats. It was suggested that I leave but I wasn't expelled. They asked me what I wanted to do. I hated it there but I thought better the devil you know, so asked if I could stay. I promised that I would try harder to behave and I did mostly. I just got on with things and muddled through. I tried my best for a little while on and off.

The thing is, I can look back now. I used to solely blame the teachers for not making the lessons interesting. I didn't care about any of it. It was all so dull. I wasn't stupid but I was lazy. Every now and again I'd think, right, I need to sort myself out here and try really hard. I quite liked Geography for example, but the teacher was so fucking dull. Imagine a bearded Open University type with a patch on his elbows and you'll get the idea. Anyway, I handed in my assignment. I'd spent ages on it, and wrote it all out nice and neatly. When it came back to me, I was looking forward to receiving top marks. I got a zero. When I queried it, he told me that I'd cheated or copied it. I was so angry. I just didn't bother after that. Now I realise that what I did, although it wasn't cheating, was nearly as bad. It showed that I *could* do the work if I tried. Most of the time I didn't. I either messed around or got beaten up. Like I say, a bad combination really!

Boris was even worse but I do at least have a funny story about that. I'm trying to keep it light!

There was a boy at school called Paul who ran a punk fanzine. Rumour had it that he was sent to the headmaster to receive the cane. As an aside, Boris had about 6 or so different types of cane, with varying flexibility. I reckon he was probably a wrong 'un looking back. The story went that Paul threatened him by pretending to throw him out of the window. I have met Paul in recent years at punk gigs and he said that this wasn't true. What was true though, was that he had found out where he lived, and went over there one evening to have it out with him. Verbally and physically if necessary. His son, who coincidentally was head boy, funny that, opened the door and asked him what he wanted. He said that he needed to speak to his dad and burst through. There he was, slumped on the couch having had too much whiskey. I asked him what happened next. He said that he was offered some whiskey and ended up getting very drunk, had a good talk and just walked home! I wished he'd smacked him one personally. I've never met anyone since who had such an air of nastiness about them. Not even close. A truly horrible specimen.

In my second year, I went into myself and got obsessed with Gary Numan and Tubeway Army. In fact, obsessed isn't strong enough really. It took over my life. I was more than obsessed. There had been a rumour going around that this new kid a couple of years above me, John Webb, was Gary Numan's brother, so eventually I asked him if he was. I got a slow, disinterested "Yeeees". He must have been sick of saying it, especially if it meant grief down the line. I was made up though and said how much of a fan I was.

He only lasted about a year or two though due to the amount of bullying he also got, but it was cool to see him being picked up from school by Gary Numan's mum or dad, and sometimes even Gary himself in his Corvette Stingray would be waiting outside. Rock City studios in Shepperton, where he had his recording studio was only about a mile away. It was so cool to see him revving up the Vette and speeding off down the road. I would watch on in disbelief. In fact, I remember Jeremy, a prefect who we used to car share with as he lived down our road in Ashford. He mentioned that he'd heard John on the public payphone in the hall talking to Gary. John was telling him about the hassle he was getting. Gary was angry and was going to come down to the school and have it out with the individuals. John had to calm him down saying "No, please don't. You'll only make it worse for me." John didn't stay long after that.

Imagine that though. It's 1979/1980 and at the height of his success, Gary Numan storms into his brother's school and has it out with the bullies like a cartoon superhero. He would've probably been arrested and on the news. Just as well that John talked him out of it really.

The last memory I have of that place is heading up the stairs for my English Language O level exam. I was actually quite looking forward to it as English was the only subject that I was ok at, as you didn't really have to revise. Needless to say, I got a pasting by Winterbaum on the stairs for no reason at all, checked in to the exam with scuffed up hair, a torn and bloody shirt, and obviously in quite a state mentally too. No questions were asked how I was or what had happened. I was just shown where to sit and get on with it. I think I somehow scraped a C.

It's amazing that I've turned out as well rounded and normal as I am. That last bit is supposed to be ironic! I'm not trying to come across as "poor me" or anything. I'm just writing down what happened. I remember thinking one day though that I'd just had enough. I climbed out of my bedroom window, legs dangling and looked down. I didn't want to die; I just didn't want to live like this. Plus, it wasn't that high. I'd probably have just sprained an ankle or something!

It was a fleeting moment and cowardice probably made me hoist myself back into the room.

Let's finish this bit on a positive note. There was one good experience from secondary school. I was in the 3rd year, and I went to France with the school. Most of the kids that I went with were ok actually. There was a group of about 5 of us who tolerated each other and none of the bullies were there. None of the ringleaders anyway. Apart from having to eat horse for dinner, it wasn't too bad. You could buy bangers (the little fireworks, not the sausages) in most newsagents. There is always a festival of some kind going on in France, so they were readily available. A few of us bought some and had fun with them. It was quite funny, because one of the kids wasn't the brightest. We were in this shop and the roly-poly shopkeeper was keeping an eye on us, so that we didn't steal anything. Very wise probably. This kid said something like,

"Look at that fat cow staring at us."

You can guess the reply.

"I can speak English you know!"

We ran out as fast as we could giggling away as schoolboys do.

Three of us decided to club together and buy one big, fuck off banger that we'd seen. This thing was like 2 sticks of dynamite taped together. We just had to have it. Surprisingly, there were no questions asked when we bought it. Of course, we couldn't wait to set it off but it had to be out of the way and in the right place.

It was now early evening and we decided to find a quiet bit of the high street in order to let it off. There wasn't anyone about so it seemed like a good time. Myself and someone else hid out of the way, whilst another lad, lit the thing and ran over to us. We were really excited but waited and waited and waited. Nothing.

"Are you sure you lit it?"

"Yes, of course I" ----------------------------------

BAAAANNNNGGGGGG!!!!!!!!!!!!!!!!!!!!!!!

This thing went off echoing all around the concrete high street. It was ridiculously loud. We stayed hidden, peeping out when we suddenly realised that he'd let the bloody thing off outside the bank. The alarms went off. They were nearly as loud as the firework. We ran away to the sounds of sirens in the background, but we got away with it. Phew. That, pretty much was school. The best days of your life apparently.

Not surprisingly, I didn't go on to further education and I won't bore you with the jobs I've had since leaving school, but they were mostly mundane temporary jobs.

Before I frequented The Royal Hart, I used to sneak into my brother's bedroom when he was out and use his CB Radio. Remember them? It was great for me. I could reinvent myself as I lived about 6 miles away from school, and got to know a few new people. OK, one of them ended up being a paedo but other than that he was alright! I used to go around to his house quite regularly to watch TV, play videos etc. He put on a blue movie once and asked me if he could do something inappropriate.

I said "No!" I ran out and never went back. I occasionally saw him walking his dog years later and left him to it.

I got to know a Brummie called Adrian on the CB who I mentioned earlier. He had just moved down to Ashford with his mum and stepdad. I used to hang around with him messing about with his car and motorbike etc.

It would often end up with us sniffing petrol or glue in his mum's garage. Not recommended but we were young and foolish. Now I'm old and foolish.

We were going to start a business that I named "Fast Forward." It was a wedding video company. Well, it would've been but we only did one wedding. We hired a camera (they were the price of a family car back then) and were filming the couple getting married in the church. We were giggling trying to be quiet behind the scenes. I think he filmed some of it with the lens cap still on and that set us off! That was the end of our business but we did get to drink plenty of free sherry and get paid. I think most of it went on the camera hire. We did become friends though, and it was through Adrian that we started to go down The Royal Hart when I was 18 in 1985.

We're Going Down

The Pub

The early days of going down The Hart are really fuzzy. I remember that Adrian had already started going down there so he knew a few people already. Some he'd been in contact with through the CB radio. I started to get to know people through knowing him. I had never been a pub person. My parents never went to the pub when I was little and it just wasn't part of my upbringing at all. I wasn't sure what to expect. I guess I'd been a bit sheltered. Most of the people were easy to talk to though, and I kind of took a back seat at first as I weighed up the various situations.

One thing I do remember though, is that I got drunk really quickly. I remember trying my hardest to try and act sober, as I thought that the hardened drinkers were used to it and never got pissed. How wrong I was!

I really enjoyed the social side of it and became friends with some of the alternative music types down there. I had, and I guess still do, have a pretty good knowledge of music. Especially on the alternative side of things, so that might have been my way in. People would ask me questions and mostly I could give them an answer. Sometimes it would even be correct! I'm still friends with most of them to this day despite some of us living miles away from each other.

It was an average sized pub split into two halves. The public bar and the lounge bar. The lounge was more for families and people who risked eating the food. This was long before gastro pubs became a thing. To simplify it, I would say that the lounge bar was more for white collar workers, and the public bar was more for blue collar workers, but not always. If you were brave, there was always a sweaty cheese roll in cellophane that appeared to have been there from the mid-70s. I don't remember anyone ever eating in the public bar. Oh actually, there was one guy. We called him "Houdi-Elbow" or Houdi for short because he looked like the Tiswas character of the same name. He always dressed in the same clothes with green jumper and grey slacks. He used to turn up on his bicycle. He was podgy and had thick rimmed glasses and bicycle clips. Not a good look. He was a bit strange and always had a cooked dinner in there. Even if it was rammed and full of smoke which it invariably was, as everyone smoked back then. He'd only ever have a couple of pints, annoyingly hover over to you at the fruit machine or jukebox, eat his dinner and go. Anyway, back to the pub. When you walked in, the pool table was right in front of you and the bar just to the left of it. There was seating by the window opposite the bar, where Richard would invariably fall asleep! Richard and John would often pop out for a puff.

When you walked in, to the left there were more tables and chairs, another big window and a dart board by the loos. Very annoying when playing. I learnt more maths playing darts than I ever did at school. The other thing was, when someone would walk in, they'd get the stare. Even if you were a regular, but especially if God forbid, you were someone new. It was good for keeping the dickheads away though –well, mostly!

The floor was always sticky. All true pubs were, and there was a slice of cucumber stuck on the ceiling for as long as I can remember, courtesy of Dave I believe. When the guvnor decided every few years that the place needed a lick of paint to cover over the yellow, nicotine-stained walls and ceiling, the cucumber just got painted over!

The staff would come and go but the old girl, Shirl was a diamond. I'm sure this was done everywhere, but every so often, if your pint was nearly finished, you could ask her for a half and she'd pretty much top it up. Good old Shirl.

I suppose I should tell you about some of the early characters in the pub. It was great because there were so many different types of people. George, however, was something else. He looked like he was dressed by his mum despite him probably being about 30 at the time. He was diminutive and always had greasy hair and a pullover on over a shirt and white vest. Even in the middle of Summer it would be vest, shirt, jumper and coat. He was harmless enough but you didn't want to get stuck with him, or he'd bore the pants off of you. The funniest thing I remember was when he came back from his holiday to Spain or somewhere. He said that he nearly didn't get to have his holiday because the plane got stuck in mid-air due to these air pockets. Air pockets!!!!!

A few people were egging him on to carry on with his story and of course, it got more and more fanciful. Passengers complaining because they wanted to get down for the holiday they were missing out on, but oh no – air pockets.

"We were stuck up there for 3 days!"

Bless him, the more he lied the funnier it became. He had a heart of gold though because he said to Graham.

"I knew it was your birthday coming up so I got you something."

Graham unwrapped this parcel and it was a tankard. A lot of the regulars used to drink from their own tankards that you'd leave behind the bar after every session. It really was a bygone era. Graham looked at it and said thankyou to George but then he noticed something. On the side, it was engraved with the name "Ken." When he questioned him if he knew his name was Graham, George said,

"Yes, of course I know you're Graham but they didn't have any with 'Graham' on and as your uncle is called Ken, I thought that was the next best thing."

The whole pub cracked up. It was a real "Trigger" moment. He just didn't get why it was so funny. I guess nowadays he'd be classified as being on the spectrum, but it was a thoughtful thing to do. Silly sod.

Another good old character was Jack. An old boy who was short, stick thin, and always had a smile on his face. He just loved a pint, a bet, and a fag. If he wasn't in the pub, he could be found in the bookies. He lived in a flat just around the back of the pub nearby and was retired. It was a bit like Andy Capp sometimes. If he didn't go home for his dinner, Dot, his missus, would turn up, not with a rolling pin but she'd give him some well-deserved ear bashing. He'd end up buying her a drink or two and they would end up staying another hour or so. When Jack won big on the racing, he'd buy the whole pub a drink and do a little dance grinning from ear to ear. I can still see it. This was a rare occasion unfortunately. They had a grown-up son, Ian who also drank down the Hart. He was a really nice guy too who sadly passed away completely out of the blue, from adult cot death I believe. He had just got a promotion and his whole life was ahead of him. Life can be so cruel. Jack and Dot were never the same again bless them.

I do remember the funeral though. Iain (who had loads of nicknames, Uncle Tubbles, Fatty, Bigness or just plain gay Iain) is still a good mate to this day. He was doing a bit of courier work on his days off from his main job. What he didn't know though, was that Simon, one of his flat mates, had painted on the side of his little van. Simon was and probably still is the biggest joker I've ever known. Dares, wind ups etc, he was your man. The van was always parked against the wall, and he painted on that side so that Iain wouldn't see it immediately. It had been left there from the previous afternoon.

In big bold letters it read: -

"FATTY'S COURIERS

NEW YORK, LONDON, PARIS, STANWELL!"

Iain got in to his van without noticing the embellishment and drove up to the cemetery. He went in with the rest of us and it was a very sad affair as you might expect. I think it was the first funeral I'd ever been to actually. It was only when Iain went back to his van that he saw it. He was mortified as relatives and other parties would've seen it on their way out. He knew straight away.

"Simon – you bastard!"

"Don't worry, it's washable!"

That gives you a flavour of what it was like over the years. No-one was safe.

One of the people I got to know was Paul. I'm still friends with him now although he lives in Spain. Paul was just different. We had a similar taste in music and he'd been going down the pub about 5 years longer than me. The first time I met him, he was drinking a pint of cider (which in itself was quite unusual back then) with a bitter top. How he came up with this concoction I still don't know but it was weird. When the bitter top was put in, it would create this chemical reaction like little sperms or something floating about. He seemed to enjoy it though followed by a red wine chaser. No-one drank wine in the public bar. I always liked Paul. He made his own rules and was an individual. Here are a few stories about Paul that either he has told me, I have witnessed or I've been told about.

1/ He got dropped off home one night after having a skinful (assume that all these anecdotes in this book are due to the person having had a skinful – it'll save me writing it out each time)

He'd been at the front door for ages and after a while, John jumped out of the car to see what he was doing.

"I can't get in." he goes.

"Bloody key!"

It was then, that John noticed him trying to get in to the lock of his front door with a 50 pence piece!

2/ Paul used to wear black DMs and tight jeans. He crashed into bed only to wake up in the morning with his jeans off but his boots still on. He must've carefully taken off his boots, followed by his jeans, and then put the boots back on which would've taken ages lacing them back up, and then gone to sleep!

3/ It's at this point that I really hope Paul isn't reading this. Sorry Paul, it's just that I remember these stories so well. He woke up one morning at the bottom of the stairs when the post landed on his head! It then took him a while before he realised where he was and retraced his steps from the previous night. He noticed loads of black marks down the wall by the side of the bannisters. He must have fallen down the stairs, scuffed said black boots on the wall on the way down, and smashed into the front door and knocked himself out. He came around when the letters landed on his bonce!

4/ OK, last one. He was at a house party and it was time to leave. I imagine the early hours of the morning. If he went left, he would've been home in 5 minutes or so. He turned right, walked a mile or 2 down the by-pass and into Staines. This would normally take a good half an hour. The state he was in it was probably double that. Eventually, he got pulled over by the boys in blue.

"Where are you going?" they said.

"Er, I'm trying to get to Ashford!" says Paul.

"You're going the wrong way."

"Oh right, can you give me a lift then?"

"No, we bloody well can't. We're not a taxi service. I think we'll stick you in the cell overnight to sober up."

He managed to talk them out of it and eventually got home by sunrise.

It was always a good night if Paul was down the pub.

Sometimes I'd go to his house. It was just him and his mum living there at that time. Upstairs he had an old reel to reel recorder, electric guitar and a couple of basic synths, a drum machine and the hi-fi. I remember watching him once. He was flicking through radio stations until he found something interesting. He eventually recorded the presenter reading out the news. He clipped it to an interesting bit of the newsreader saying,

"A French aircraft disaster" or something like that. He then integrated it with this drum loop, guitar and synths. It was great. Like a Pop Will Eat Itself or Big Audio Dynamite instrumental. Paul joined a few bands and we would go and see him play but none were really my cup of tea. I much preferred the stuff he did on his own. When he said goodbye to his mum he'd put on a Scottish accent.

"Reet, see ya later" in a broad Glaswegian accent. I thought he was pissing about the first time he did it, but I soon realised that he'd put on the accent to speak to his mum. I've since seen other people do things similar.

There was another bloke from the pub. An older guy called Alfie. He'd always be on his own but after a few pints, he'd start singing (in a pub style). None of us ever recognised the songs. We'd often tell him to shut the fuck up but it didn't stop him. On and on he'd sing is his slurred monotonous tone. Irritating but quite amusing looking back.

It's at this point that I've been deliberating whether to put some of this stuff in but sod it, I'm going to because I am just reporting on what went on. Now, The Royal Hart, I think it's pretty fair to say was not always politically correct! There were lots of nicknames for people. More often than not, these would come about by finding a weakness or a difference in someone and exploiting it.

I'm going to give you an idea by naming a few that I can remember. Obviously, I was Spanner, Paul was Kilty (Scottish connection), you had Stav as he looks like Stavros from Kojak, FB for Keith (fat bastard), Big Roy who used to do Elvis impressions, even when nobody wanted him to, Tony The Wop (self-explanatory), Jock who started calling Craig, Geldof when he grew his hair long and straggly and Mickey was called Houndy to name a few. Not sure why he was called Houndy actually.

Update, he's just texted me and I never knew this……….

Mickey: - "It was bank holiday Monday and I was with Goatie, Brewer, Cromo and Richard at Virginia Waters FC. We decided to go to one of the local pubs and it was karaoke night. When you went in, you got a ticket with a

54

song on it. Mine was Hound Dog by Elvis Presley. I guess I
sang it – badly, but it got a laugh and the name Houndy just
stuck."

There was a young kid called Darren who I think had MS.
Due to his condition he was known as Shaky. He loved a
game of pool but you can guess the number of times he
accidentally knocked a ball. Some meanies would shout
"foul" and take 2 shots! Mind you, I could understand why
if it was on a Sunday. There would be about 30 names on
the board, so if you lost, you'd had it. There was gay Iain,
otherwise known as Uncle Tubbles, as previously
mentioned, Cyclops (she only had one eye and wasn't
aware of her nickname to be fair) and Basher who I think
got his name from the way he played football. Later on,
The Royal Hart had a few football teams at certain times.

Now, I know there's some well dodgy names there. What I
will say though, without getting too political, is that
everyone was honest. It wasn't often that you'd call

someone something behind their back. We'd say it to their face. Sometimes you'd get a bit of stick and other times you'd give it. None of this snowflake generation nonsense. I'll give you an example which happened pretty regularly and always made everyone laugh.

Sometimes Jock would be in the pub and Uppy, who was of Indian descent I think, would walk in. Jock in his thick Glaswegian accent would shout,

"Fuck off Uppy, ya Paki bastard!"

Without flinching for a second, Uppy would reply in a football chanting way,

"I'd rather be a Paki than a Jock!"

More often than not they would be at the bar having a pint and a laugh and it was all good natured. Sometimes an outsider would witness it and not know what to make of it, which just made it even more funny. Can you imagine it happening now?

I guess the world has moved on and it's different times. Probably for the best.

Uppy had to have an operation due to an illness and ended up with a colostomy bag fitted. It didn't seem to bother him as he'd still boom his infectious laugh "Woo hoo hoo hoo" Think Frank Bruno only not as deep but twice as loud. Whenever he found something even remotely funny, you'd hear it again. Woo hoo hoo hoo! He even carried on with his forward roly polys when he got a bit pissed.

"Make way, make way!" and he'd run and do 2 or 3 forward roly polys in front of the bar. Nutter. What wasn't quite so welcome was when he'd sometimes let out some excess air from his colostomy bag. Eugh! It was disgusting.

One other thing about Uppy that I remember is when The Royal Hart football team got to the final of the cup competition. It was played in the Cobham/ Leatherhead area and a few of us travelled by coach to see it. There was a bar and you were allowed to watch the game by the side of the pitch. Simon who was playing in the match came over at one point mid game and drank my pint in one. The Royal Hart was a great place, but it did have a bit of a reputation. The referee was obviously a "homer." And it started getting ridiculous. He gave the opposition everything and us nothing. It was blatant cheating. Uppy wasn't happy about this, so mid-way through the second half, after another outrageous decision, he ran on to the pitch and threw the rest of his pint in the direction of the referee. This didn't go down too well. He got sent off, even though he was only a supporter and I think in the end we lost 1-0. The team also got a hefty fine. Not surprising really as it turned out that the ref was on the committee.

Not everyone had a nickname though. There was a guy called Kane. He eventually married one of the girls who used to frequent the pub. Her name was Tracey. That was all well and good but Kane's surname was Tracy so she became Tracey Tracy!

I'm sure there were loads more nicknames for other people. Almost everyone had one. There was Geordy Normy. He once told me that he was watching Newcastle play at St James' Park, when he was introduced to this girl called 'Skunker'. Normy asked her why she was called that other than the fact that Newcastle play in black and white. She told him because her name is Nancy. Skunker Nancy – genius!

Everything and everyone was fair game. I'm of the opinion that you can make a joke out of anything. Sometimes the outrageous nature of a joke is what makes it funny. What I personally can't stand, is crude or distasteful jokes when they are *not* funny. I guess it's a fine line sometimes and what one person finds funny, another reports you to the police! I won't mention any names but Syd was terrible. Funny but terrible. He, like myself was a massive Ian Dury fan. Unfortunately, Ian Dury had passed away the same week that we met up to go to a funeral, for a regular down the pub who had also sadly died. She had been ill for some time and was also disabled. Everyone was of course solemn when we met up at The Hart to go to the funeral, including her boyfriend and some of her family. Syd came up to me and whispered into my ear,

"It's been a bad week for raspberries!"

For fuck's sake, I couldn't very well laugh – everyone looking so sad. I had to pinch myself until it hurt. I mean he loved Ian Dury and was gutted about that and the person from The Hart who had died too. I won't say who it was as I don't want to upset any family members who may read this. It wasn't meant as disrespect, it's just that he just had to tell me the gag. Better out than in.

I did get Syd back though a few years later with a similar joke. We all met up at The North Star in Staines. We'd arranged to get a train to Richmond to see The Specials at

Kew Gardens. It was early. Myself and Syd were having a chat and our first couple of beers of the day. The TVs were on with the sound down. It was Wimbledon fortnight and they were showing the wheelchair doubles. I called over,

"Ere Syd, I thought Wimbledon was supposed to be famous for strawberries, not raspberries."

He spat out his drink.

"You bastard!"

I was thinking that Syd wouldn't normally get upset at a joke like that. Then I realised why he had that response. He was annoyed that he hadn't thought of it first!

Of course, I am not being nasty or mocking disabled people. It's a joke. From my experience, most people who pretend to be appalled and want to ban everything are not the people who are directly affected. It's normally white liberals who want to save the world. Yoghurt knitters as the radio broadcaster, Mike Dickin used to put it so eloquently. I miss him.

I'll give you an example. A mate of mine, Mark used to tell me this great story. He had a mate who ended up in a wheelchair having lost both of his legs. I think it was due to diabetes. Amazingly, he just got on with things and somehow kept his sense of humour. A few of them went out for the day to the beach in the middle of summer. He slowly managed to walk towards the sea. When he was close enough, he sat down and took off his prosthetic legs and chucked them to one side. He was having a great time splashing about. After a while, he began crawling out of the sea towards everyone on the beach shouting at the top of his voice "Sharks, Sharks!" scaring everyone shitless. Quality. That is why you shouldn't worry about offending people with a joke. As long as it's funny.

It's Christmas!

I'd been going down the Hart for about a year now, and I knew that Christmas Eve was a big deal. In fact, it was the highlight of the year.

The pool table would get covered over and moved to one side, the place was decorated with by some of the regulars a week or so before, and everyone would turn up. The pub did get a bit of a bad name in later years but there was hardly ever any trouble. Having said that, the first Christmas Eve that I was there, it pretty much ended when there was a fight – between two women. They were fighting over some bloke. I didn't really know them. It was quite comical though and I'd already had my quota of booze so I was quite happy to walk home after a brilliant night. I was about half way down the high street when a few lads were kicking a ball about.

"Do you wanna join in?" they shouted. It seemed like a good idea at the time so we ended up playing football in the high street, stopping as the odd car went by. We ended up having a 2 a side on the tiny roundabout at the end of the road. It was such a laugh and so random. Cars were slowing down, people shouting out "Merry Christmas!" beeping, and we were having a very drunk game of a new sport called roundabout football! It was like something out of an updated Dickensian novel.

Eventually, a police car patrolled by and they put a stop to it. They saw the funny side as it was all good humoured and we begrudgingly moved on. It was a good laugh though and a real buzz getting a reaction from the drivers going by. As a footnote, I recently found out, over 35 years later, that the guys playing football were friends of a friend!

I think it was the following Christmas Eve that I got so drunk, that whilst walking home, I fell into a hedge. I remember getting stuck and couldn't get out. I don't know why but I remember talking to said hedge and thinking to myself, I must be really pissed if I'm talking to a hedge! It was a few years later when I noticed a lyric to a Pogues song about talking to a wall whilst paralytic when I thought, bloody hell, I was as pissed as Shane McGowan that Christmas Eve. How apt.

There was a tradition down the pub leading up to Christmas which I didn't know about. Normally, on a Saturday in December all the blokes would go Christmas shopping. The first I heard about it was when Paul asked me if I wanted to go. I didn't really see the point in traipsing all the way into London just to pay exorbitant prices and lug it all back, so I said that I wasn't bothered.

On this particular Saturday afternoon there was a good crowd of us. Paul asked me if I was sure as I'd be on my own once they'd all gone. I thought he was winding me up until everyone started fucking off. Bollocks.

"OK – I'm coming" and I caught them all up as we walked over to the station to get the train in to Waterloo. It was only once we got to Leicester Square and Covent Garden, when I thought we haven't actually done any shopping, yet we must have been to 4 or 5 pubs.

"When are we doing the Christmas shopping?" I naively asked. Everyone started laughing and it was explained that about 5 years ago, someone said shall we go Christmas shopping to get away from the wives and girlfriends for a day. Of course, there was no shopping ever involved. Here they were, still just about getting away with it all these years later. This tradition has finally run its course after 40 odd years although never say never again.

With Christmas shopping, something would always happen. Some years were better than others, but it was always a good crack.

The first few are a bit of a blur, but the first early one I remember is when there was only about 6 of us. We normally went to London but sometimes we'd go to Richmond, Twickenham or Windsor. Always a train ride away. On this occasion we went to London. It was always the same start. Waterloo, walk over the bridge and into the edge of Covent Garden and Leicester Square. We walked into this pub. It was probably the second one of the day, but we'd only had a couple of beers. It was pretty busy so we split and sat down for a bit at different tables. Myself and Mark asked this old guy if he minded us sitting down with him on his table. He seemed ok with it and we all started chatting small talk. Completely out of the blue, and to this day I don't know why, Mark started talking out loud what most people would just think in their head. I reckon he had temporary Tourette's for a moment. He said to this bloke,

"'Ere, you ain't half got a big nose, haven't ya?"

I couldn't believe it. I started laughing which made Mark laugh. The elderly gentlemen didn't quite see it that way. He got up to leave but as he did so, he gave Mark quite a hard slap across the head. I was still laughing.

"What did you say that for?"

"I don't know, it just came out. I was just staring at it and couldn't keep it in."

I mean, he did have a big hooter but even so. I've often asked Mark about this over the years and he still has no idea why he said it.

I'm trying to think of other things that have happened. Sometimes, we would start off at The Wellington in Waterloo. The Great Train Robber, Buster Edwards would often be selling flowers outside on his stall. He popped in

68

for a quick whiskey once. He started to leave but changed his mind mid walk. "Fuck it, give me another" he said, downed it and went back out into the cold back to his stall. A couple of years later, he was found hanged in a garage around the corner.

We used to get well hammered and I don't remember much so the next few stories are of more recent times. The last 10 or 15 years probably.

There was one time when we went to Windsor for a change. It wasn't one of the best expeditions but we were all up for it. Having lined our stomachs with a hearty full English breakfast, we jumped on the train, only about 6 stops to Windsor. We were chatting away probably excited about the laugh we'd have later in the day. Dave was recounting some story or other and we were all chipping in with the usual bollocks. I suddenly realised that the train hadn't moved for about 10 minutes. I mentioned this, we all looked over at the platform – we were in Windsor, the end of the line! If we'd sat there a minute or two longer, the train would've started on its way back. You probably had to be there but it was most amusing.

When we got to the high street, after a few beers, we noticed a massive 30 foot tall Christmas tree right near the castle. John dared this guy Tony to climb it. I mean Tony is a big lad but he'd have a go at anything after a couple of beers. John of course knew this so without any warning, up he started to go. Knocking off bits of tinsel and baubles as he went. He got about two thirds of the way up which was pretty impressive to be fair. Then of course he couldn't get down. I think he'd sobered up. We were all laughing at him as he gingerly manoeuvred himself back down from the outsized conifer, like a cat who'd had second thoughts.

There was another time when we ended up in Leicester Square. No matter where we started in London, we always seemed to end up in bloody Leicester Square. There was a temporary, really high fairground ride outside the Capital

Radio building. It was one of those things that has 2 carriages and spins on its axis. I was up there with the other Mark whilst the others waited. It was only when we started spinning around (much faster and much higher than it bloody well appeared on the ground) that I said to Mark,

"I don't know why I went on this. I fucking hate heights."

With the cold wind whizzing past, Mark said,

"I know, me too!" and we laughed.

Then it stopped – phew. Only a temporary pause from the turmoil though, as it then started to go backwards. My 4 pints were starting to request a vacation but I managed to keep them down and we got off, legs turning to jelly. I really do not like fairground rides. What was I thinking? Still, the adrenalin had now kicked in and we were on our way to having a good evening.

Sometimes, on occasion, you would get that really Christmassy feeling. Not often, but sometimes. Dave was with us on this occasion. We were well oiled by now and we found this traditional London pub. I got myself some roasted chestnuts from a vendor outside, who had one of those brazier things that looked like a hot dog stand from episodes of Starsky And Hutch. It was freezing outside. I think there was even the odd flurry of snow which was rare for London. I had chestnuts, trying not to burn my fingers as I peeled them and then went in to the pub. Dave, who loved a good sing song followed me in. Dave was great company, especially at Christmas. Anyway, he dashed straight to the loos. Meantime, there was another punter who noticed a piano in the corner of the pub so he started playing and singing some Chas and Dave tunes on the old joanna. He played a couple of songs and we all sang along. It really was a magical moment. Dave came in from the bogs and missed it all. He would've loved it and I'm sure we'd still be there now if he'd known. Oh well, they say less is more.

God, I know I've missed so much out. There was a recent incident where we were having a last drink outside under these big umbrellas. We were about to go into Chinatown to soak it up a bit before going home. This was often a good way to finish off the day.

It really was starting to rain a bit harder. This attractive young French woman and her partner strolled up. They were probably outside because they were smoking. He went in to get them a couple of drinks. Dave went over to her, and in his broad, cockney type accent he innocently asked,

"Are you wet?"

We all looked at each other as if to say you can't say that. Then we started giggling like school boys. Now Dave could be as crude as the next bloke, in fact more so quite often, but on this occasion, he was being straight. He just didn't get it.

"What, I just asked if she was wet?" he carried on. By now, I think she had even cottoned on to what we were laughing at. Dave was the only one who wasn't laughing. Then her partner came back and rather wisely, we moved on.

Speaking of Dave, about 25 years prior to that, we all decided to go down The Crooked Billet in Staines for a Christmas drink and evening meal. There was probably a deal on, because we wouldn't normally go out anywhere for a meal, except the Kismet which I'll get to later.

There were maybe 6 to 10 of us in there, and we were seated upstairs overlooking from the internal balcony. We were slowly getting a bit sozzled and had started eating our meal when the Sally Army came in and started playing festive carols. It would probably be lovely now, but back then it was annoying. Dave rather cheekily lobbed over a small roast potato and I saw it land down the guy's tuba. This then became a game. We ended up chucking all manner of things down that poor bloke's tuba. Peanuts, peas. All sorts. I bet he had a job cleaning it out the next

day. It carried on working though. Hark! The Herald

Pissheads Fling! Speaking of the Kismet.

The Kismet

Where do I even begin? The Kismet was the name of the curry house just over the road from The Hart. I wonder why they're called curry houses? You get a pizza parlours, fish and chip shops and curry houses. Very strange.

The Kismet was where you would go at the weekend in order to drink more beer and talk more bollocks after the pub had shut. If you were flush, maybe in the week too. You had to eat also, so it wasn't long before I became enamoured with curries. Not everyone felt the same. There was Ray. I'm sure he will pop up throughout this book as he was a lot of things.

Charismatic, funny, ignorant, selfish, – in fact, pretty much any adjective you'd like to throw at him. I got on really well with him but some people quite rightly didn't. You wouldn't invite him round to your house. He would relieve you of some of your worldly goods. I'll get back to the Kismet in a minute. Before I mention how I got to know Ray, I feel that I should set the scene. He would skulk around, looking miserable, and a bit cat like. Later on in the evening, he would lighten up and be very funny. He was the sort of person that wouldn't wave back at someone on a boat as they gently went by. You know the sort.

He was a regular, but I didn't really know Ray well, until most of the pub descended to this warehouse party somewhere near Heathrow Airport. Only half of us had tickets but Ray said

"Stay with me and you'll be alright."

He was older than me, a long distance lorry driver who'd been around a bit and seemed to know what he was doing. Just as well as we soon realised that the bouncers on the door were pretty stringent. We hung around outside for a while. It was still light and Ray noticed that this girl's car wouldn't start. I still hadn't cottoned on but he said,

"Quick!" so we ran over and asked her if she wanted a push. All three of us gave her a push, the car powered up, and off she gratefully went, right by the entrance to the warehouse. I thought that we'd just done a nice thing.

Ray then said,

"Follow me."

We did. The three of us breezed past the bouncers on the door when one of them said,

"Where are you lot going?" Ray, quick as a flash replied,

"We just popped out to get our friend's car started."

Genius – in we went.

I mean, the party was shit and we didn't stay long but that's not the point. To me, that summed Ray up perfectly. He was doing a girl a favour, me and my mate a favour, but all

of it was a pretence for the devious behaviour of him,

getting something for nothing.

Back to The Kismet, one of the funniest things ever, and

there were many, involved Ray. As I say, he was an

articulated lorry driver. That's not to say that he was a lorry

driver who spoke well, he drove an HGV with 2 sections

but I'm guessing that you worked that out for yourself. He

was also a country and western fan. I hated C&W at the

time. Still do really except for Johnny Cash. Mind you

apart from Killed By Death by Motorhead, it's a C&W

song that has my favourite title. You're The Reason Our

Kids Are Ugly by Conway Twitty and Loretta Lynn. Don't

listen to it – it's shit! Anyway, back to Ray. A friend of his

also got him into The Stranglers. He loved The Model and

The Lovecats by Kraftwerk and The Cure too. It's funny

what you remember. We would often sing out (very) loud,

random Stranglers lyrics down the pub when we'd had too many. "Making love to, the Mersey Tunnel, with a sausage in my hand, have you ever been to Liverpool?" On this occasion, I think it was a Sunday night. Myself, Ray and another Ray just got in to the Kismet in time before it shut. We ordered a couple of buds and a curry. Ray had been on it all day and never ate curry. On the odd occasion when he did go in there, he always had omelette and chips. As soon as we ordered, Ray's eyes were closing – he'd had enough. Myself and the other Ray would poke him into life every now and again for our entertainment. Eventually the food arrived. We ordered more beer except Ray whose face fell into the omelette and chips. The waiter said,

"Oh no, it's hot, should we do something?"

We said "No, you're better off leaving him, trust us."

We ate our curry still talking and laughing, every now and then pointing at Ray with his head in his dinner. When we finished, it was nearly midnight and well past closing time. We paid our part of the bill and the waiter started clearing the table. Having had his head planted in the omelette and chips for a good half an hour now, the waiter disturbed him to move the plate. He lifted up his face with omelette peeling off his skin like something out of an 80s slasher film. You couldn't tell where the omelette stopped and the skin began! His face was burnt red underneath and he said quietly but menacingly,

"LEAVE IT!"

It was so funny; the waiter was trying to explain that they were closed.

"I DON'T CARE – LEAVE IT!"

He was left to slowly eat the cold omelette and chips. The poor waiters did get some bad treatment, but it was so funny.

I don't think I ever gave the waiters any stick. At least not on purpose. There was a time though when there were a few of us on one table, and a few others that we knew on another. Most of them were in the college covers band Kabuki Smiles as previously mentioned. They were brilliant and we used to follow them about regularly playing live. My old mate Adrian was now the lead singer and he was with me on our table. It had been another excellent evening and we were all in high spirits. The next bit is quite embarrassing but also went down into local folklore as me setting light to the curry house!

What happened was, whilst we were waiting for our food, we all put those paper serviettes on our heads like Christmas cracker crowns for some strange reason. Of course, I didn't stop there – I decided to fold another one in half, cut out two eyeholes out and make a "brilliant" Batman type mask. I was doing by best Batman impression when everyone was laughing. I thought it was ok but not

that great. Still, if it's getting a laugh, carry on – so I did;
that is, until I realised that my crown was on fire. That's
what they were laughing at, the bastards.

"Shit, my heads alight!" I shouted as I threw the paper hat
off. It fell to the ground and I berated Adrian for being a
twat for setting it on fire, when I realised the bottom of the
tablecloth had now caught alight. I must admit that I froze.
I was already stressed out by now. The flames were
growing bigger and bigger until one of the waiters noticed
and ran over shouting and screaming at us. As he was
stamping out the flames, his flared trousers also caught
alight! He got a towel and put it out. We all got a week's
ban. I mean, it wasn't my bloody fault. For years after,
people would ask me if it was true that I started a fire in the
curry house.

On another occasion, Adrian had been in the loos for quite
a while. He was frogmarched back in as he had got stuck,

trying to do a runner, by escaping through the top window in the gents leaving me to pay. Justice!

I remember some nights were so rowdy. I do look back and cringe a little. One night we had a massive food fight. I reckon there were about 10 tables in there and everyone had joined in by the end. I think it all started the night that Dave sat down and exclaimed that he would like a bottle of wine and a whole tandoori chicken! It took him a while to get his way, but sure enough, half an hour or so later, a whole chicken was served up on a plate, "tandoorid" to within an inch of its life.

I'd never seen anything like it. I think it was the excess chicken that started the fight but I may be wrong.

There were so many great evenings that finished up in the curry house. An ongoing game was to do a runner. I was never a fan of this but sometimes you just had to join in.

The one occasion that I remember is 4 or 5 of us trying to get in because we'd done a runner the previous week. We said sorry – it was just for fun and you can add it to this week's bill.

We all sat and had a couple of pints and onion bhajis. They did the best onion bhajis in there. They were flat like beefburgers so they cooked more evenly, not like the massive round ones you get now that are cold in the middle. We also ordered our mains as well. The owner had cottoned on to us after last week and as we were nearly finished eating, he decided to lock the door. John got up and asked if he could be let out as he'd left his wallet in the car. The waiter reluctantly said "OK" and let him out. I still hadn't twigged until about 5 minutes later. The waiter came back and asked me where he was. I had to think on my feet, which is difficult at the best of times but even harder after half a dozen pints. I said,

"Bloody Hell – he's probably trying to get into my car. I've locked it. Let me go and let him in to get his wallet."

Again, reluctantly, he unlocked the door and let me out. I just about saw John right down the other end of the road and shouted at him.

"You bastard!"

He was still laughing. I ran off also and, in the end, Keith got the bill for both weeks! Not for the first time or the last. There was no way he was gonna do a runner. He liked his curry and beer too much to leave any! I'm sure we paid him back eventually – well, maybe.

Christmas Work Do's

(And Don'ts!)

Christmas work do's in the late 80s and early 90s were legendary. Not where I worked so much but my now wife's ones were brilliant. I do remember going to one of my work dos though, trying to make the effort. It was annoying as we had an invite to a place called Meadhurst in Sunbury, which was colloquially known as the BP Club as it was full of BP members, and right next door to their head office. So, myself and Lisa got to this place just outside Ashford called the Esso Club, right on the outskirts of Heathrow airport. We got there and it was dead. No atmosphere. There were about 10 people milling about and a DJ playing crap hip hop or something really loudly. I remember lasting about 5 minutes and then saying to Lisa, shall we go to the BP Club instead. She agreed. I remember phoning up for a cab on the payphone in the hallway, long before mobiles or Uber, and asking the cab office to send someone to the Esso Club, to pick us up and drop us off at the BP Club. He thought I was having a laugh and it took me a while to convince him that it wasn't a prank call!

Back to one of the weirdest evenings ever though. My wife's work do, which was just weird. It was held at one of the main hotels on the Bath Road at Heathrow. As per usual, everything was laid on. Sparkling wine, 3 course meal, more wine and even an open bar followed by cigars for the men. For most of the evening, it was business as usual. One of the old managers dancing badly with his over made-up wife; dancing with confidence rather than talent. Probably to Dancing Queen or some such.

Meanwhile, our table was getting pretty lively. Not only did we have Lisa's nutty work mate, Sandra on our table, but we also had another couple who we are friends of to this day, Diane and Gary. I may be compiling 2 work dos into one here but bear with me. I don't know what it is with me and fires at the dinner table, but somehow, Lisa's scatty mate had set the tablecloth alight. It was only a small fire though and it would've been put out easily with a glass of water. However, she decided to put it out with a glass of neat spirit – woof! Up it went. It ended up with her being covered in water as everyone drunkenly tried to help by drowning out the fire. We got up and carried on with our evening.

What a great night it was. We were having a fantastic evening, but it was coming to an end so we thought we'd be clever for once. Diane and Gary and us two, decided to get a cab at about 20 minutes to midnight to beat the rush. We were waiting by the concierge for a while, when we saw a bloke get frogmarched off with a gun taken off him. To this day, I still can't believe it but we all saw it. Nothing was mentioned about it ever. Just weird. Then, to cap it off, probably the funniest thing that I have ever seen happened. Maybe it was because we'd had a few drinks, I don't know. We had been waiting a while for the cab to turn up, and Gary was getting impatient. He decided to get up and walk outside in case it was there and maybe we couldn't see it.

He got up and walked at a good pace up to the glass doors, as an onomatopoeic 'whoosh' noise sounded as if he were on the Star Trek Enterprise, as he walked through stridently, then up to the next set of glass doors which as I'm sure you have guessed by now, were absent in their 'woosh' as at full walking pace, he clattered straight into the glass, probably leaving a perfect imprint of his "boat race" on the window as he bounced backwards into a heap on the floor. He assumed (wrongly) that these doors were locked open.

It was one of those moments where you instantly stopped what you were talking about. Myself, Lisa and Diane burst into tumultuous laughter. I'm not kidding, between the three of us, we didn't stop for a good 10 minutes. As soon as someone had just about calmed down, and composed themselves, you'd look over and your streaming eyes would meet, the shoulders would go and you'd be off again in hysterics for another minute. It was all you could do to catch your breath. It was so funny. It didn't help when Gary looked over and said,

"It's OK, I'm alright."

I think he had really hurt himself but that just made it all the funnier. What a night that was. We hardly ever mention it when we meet these days. Well, not every time at least.

Summertime

I remember we were sitting outside The Royal Hart in the summertime, just chilling out on the bench seats, when Dave and a few others, just loaded a couple of benches with the tables attached, on top of his car, and drove off to his house to use at the bbq he was having. The next day, the landlord Mick, just said,

"I want my benches back."

That was all he had to do. They were returned that evening. He wasn't happy but it was dealt with. These days, they would probably call the police and all sorts – simpler times.

Mind you, he'd also nicked a mirror from the ladies toilet on a separate occasion and had it in his hallway for years. At one of the parties he had, the main barman recognised it but nothing was said.

Sometimes a few of us would go to this beauty spot called Frensham Ponds. It was a good 30-mile drive away but it was a decent place to chill out on a sunny day.

I think I only went once. Steve who ran the newsagents opposite drove and we spent the afternoon there. It wasn't really my thing. I was still semi-gothed up in those days. Luckily, it was overcast and we came back early and made the evening session in the Hart.

I do recollect Mark telling me that he once went there, again with Steve who drove. This time Steve's brother-in-law Stu went. Now Stu was a bit of a nutter. He was and probably still is eccentric, and that coupled with the fact that he just didn't give a fuck made for some interesting incidents. There's nothing he wouldn't do. That's probably why he ended up with a glass eye although I honestly can't remember how that happened. He did tell me once but I can't remember. He would stare at you like you'd done something. It was just his eye in permanent stare mode!

Mark said they parked up in the municipal car park right by the pond. As they were getting out with cool bags loaded with lager, Stu strips off completely bollock naked on a Saturday afternoon and put on one of those old fashioned all in one men's swimsuits. He just didn't give a shit.

He was another one who could liven up an evening or sometimes go a bit too far. I remember once we were playing volleyball or something around the back of Iain's flat in-between sessions. It was a good laugh on a hot summer's day. Stu was perched right on top of a tall stepladder like he was a tennis umpire. It was very funny as he was adjudicating like he was on Centre Court at Wimbledon. After a good while, the ball inevitably went over the fence, and Rob the postman volunteered to get it. It was full of thick brambles but he said he could reach it if someone could hang on to his legs and dangle him over. He was nearly there when Stu lost patience. He climbed down from his high chair, ran towards him, and just pushed him over the fence to get it. He landed head first on to the concrete in real pain. For the rest of the time I saw Rob, he always had a chipped tooth poor bloke. He went mad trying to kill Stu and I think there was a bit of a scuffle. All very unnecessary really.

<u>Gigs (Part 1)</u>

It's difficult to know where to start with my gig going really. There will be more amusing anecdotes on my gig going throughout this book, but I feel I should start at the beginning.

My first gig was also my best, and it will never be beaten. Gary Numan, supported by SHOCK! on the last night of his 3 sold out retirement shows at Wembley Arena in 1981. It was the week before my 14th birthday, and I only managed to go because I was desperate. As I said earlier, I was an obsessive Numan fan by now and he was retiring from playing live. I noticed in the window of The Record Scene in Staines, that there was a big homemade advert written on the glass saying something like "Final Night -

Gary Numan At Wembley Tuesday April 28th – £5 Enquire Within."

As Gary was local to the area, I imagined that his mum or dad had a deal with the record shop. 10% commission or something, seeing as his dad was also Gary's manager. Anyway, to cut a long story short, I saved up for a couple of months, and bought 2 tickets, sold one to a mate at school and eventually cajoled my dad into driving us there and back. Luckily, my dad had an uncle who lived in Wembley and they'd arranged to meet at his during the gig – thanks dad.

Looking back, I was so lucky to not only live so near or I would never have gone, but also, they could've stopped selling the tickets in the record shop at any given time.

The Wembley gigs were just massive. Probably the biggest gigs held anywhere by anyone at that time.
It was a genuine "thankyou" to the fans for sticking by him, but he also wanted to go out in style. It was reported that

despite selling out all three shows, he lost £25,000 per night in 1981 due to the enormous set design. Over the three nights, that would be over a quarter of a million pounds now!

When we rolled up, I was amazed at all the Gary Numan lookalikes. There were Numan tunes blaring out of car radios. It felt like a real event. I've been to Wembley a few times since and although it's a large venue, it seemed humungous back then.

A place where we could all meet. You'd hardly ever find a Gary Numan fan back then, and here there were literally thousands. It was so exciting.

It's been well documented and there's still a dvd available of it, so I won't go through the whole gig here, but the lights were amazing. It looked like a spaceship. There were costume changes, guests, a massive cinema screen, gantries, he drove in a remote-controlled car, came down from the rafters in a lit-up cage, came up from a trap door, and endless encores. Even the sound was ridiculously loud. By reading his first autobiography some years later, he explained that when they were setting up the gear during the week, they found out that there was a disused swimming pool under the arena, so they packed it out it with extra bass speakers. When those analogue synthesizers rumbled and screamed, your whole body shook and it felt like your bones were being realigned. Talking about it really does not do it justice. Utterly mind blowing and it was too much for me to take in really. I was never the same again. Thankyou Gary Numan.

To my surprise, about 6 months later, I got a letter through from the Gary Numan Fan Club. Probably due to my proximity to Numan HQ, I was asked if I wanted to be a part of the making of a forthcoming video. Er, yes, I bloody well did!

It was to be a single written and recorded by his old backing band, who were now called Dramatis. They had asked him to sing on this particular song and there was to be a video. It was being filmed at Shepperton Studios, where he had his recording studio, Rock City. Only a mile or so from my school.

I was allowed to take one other person. Well, it had to be Ian who I went to the Wembley gig with. My dad agreed to pick us up and drive us over there after school, hang around and take us both home. I was so excited. I wanted to go straight there from school, but it was much too early. My parents said it would be much better to come home, have something to eat, and change clothes. I had to admit that that was a better idea. Even so, I kept saying that we should leave, and eventually my dad caved in and we did. When we got there, we got let through the security barrier and were told which stage to go to. I was now really nervous. The last time I saw Gary Numan, it was in the cavernous aircraft hangar that is Wembley Arena. Now, I was going to be right in front of him in this fairly small sound stage/ studio. I had suddenly become very nervous. We were the first ones there by ages. It was quite a small room with a modest stage at one end, decked out like a live concert with some basic lighting. Me and my mate were talking to each other, trying to look cool, when suddenly, Gary walks right past us in his 1930s suit. His latest image. I had seen the change of image from his solo album and single that had been released about a month earlier. He was without the jacket though and it kind of threw me at first. Looking back, I now think that he was pretending to be busy. He probably walked past, expecting us to start talking to him, but we had suddenly become mute.

I was kicking myself when about 15 minutes later, 2 girls walked in, went straight up to him and started chatting. For fuck's sake. Why was I so shy?

Despite that, as the room filled up with about 100 or so fans, it became a fantastic evening. The director told us what to do. It was supposed to look like a live gig up close near the front. We ended up getting further and further back but it was still cool. I counted the number of times that the song Love Needs No Disguise got played and mimed through. Nine in all and I now really liked the track. It was so annoying that it didn't get released for another couple of months or so after. I still love it to this day.

There was a moment in the proceedings when an old Rolls Royce came through the crowd and the band got out. I recognised the car as the same one Gary had bought for his dad. I remember tugging Russell Bell's long leather coat as he got out. He was the guitarist and main singer in Dramatis when Gary wasn't guesting. I looked up and saw the camera pointing right at me. I did my best Numan stare directly down the lens. I think I overdid it though as I stared for the next five minutes. What a knob. It never got

used. I was gutted when the video came out and I couldn't
see myself, however, now I think it's just as well.

The following year he changed his mind and did a small
tour of America, and the year after that, a full 40 date tour
of the UK. I went to all 4 nights at Hammersmith Odeon.
The last night was an added extra and was free to fan club
members. I'm pretty sure I did one of the Dominion nights
too near the end of the tour. I'd made some new friends
from Feltham via the CB radio that I mentioned previously.
The main guy was Rich but I forget who the others were.
For some reason, Feltham seemed to be a stronghold for
Numan fans, and I think that they had a bit of a local
reputation. I met some of them at The Flag which I'll
mention later. I got to know Rich and his mates quite well
for a year or so. It was pretty cool because he had a den at
the bottom of his garden, where he had a video player and a
few Numan videos amongst other things. At home, we
didn't get a video player until much later on, so it was a

good place to get my fix of The Touring Principle,

Newman Numan and of course Micromusic. I got on pretty

well with Rich and his mates and about 4 of us decided that

we would have a weekend away. I'm digressing again.

It was organised by Richard, and we were going to Warners

Holiday Camp. Hello campers! I paid my deposit and really

had no idea what to expect. It was a bit weird. I always felt

like a bit of an outsider because I came from the

comparably posh Ashford, the nice house and private

education. We got on ok but lost touch rather than ever

falling out, but I was a bit of an outsider, I guess. When we

got there (wherever there was) we quickly got ready and

had a look about. I think we all hoped we'd pull, but we got

pissed instead. The first evening's entertainment was none

other than Renee and fucking Renato. I gave Richard a load

of stick for this so he ended up giving me a drinking

challenge. Let's see who can drink the most pints. I was

always a 4 or 5 pint person with maybe a JD or two at the

end of a session on occasion, which I'd normally regret the next day. I am though, fairly competitive.

As it turned out, Renato, the chubby Brummie/ Italian bloke was quite funny as a stand up. Well, he was after the 6th pint anyway. He did get a bit fed with us going up and down for trays of beer all the time, and took the piss out of us but it was all good natured. He was nothing like he was caricatured to be in the Save Your Love video. He made a few rude jokes. I remember one.

In his put on over the top Italian accent, he went on about how he likes England.

"I lika Fuckerstone (Folkestone.) Me and Renee lika the Fuckerstone very much. (Muffled laughter)

We also alike er Fucksuck, I mean Suffuck. Suffuck is very niiice!" he continued.

"There's one a place we not a like. We not a like Nofuck."

That brought the house down. It was actually very funny which is how I remember it from all those years ago. This went on for a while, they did Save Your Love again (handy for another piss break) and myself and Rich were starting to struggle on our ninth pint. We had a mate who was counting and presumed that it was correct. We both just about finished number 10 and I asked him if he wanted another.

"I'm done" he said, so I had to buy an 11th pint to beat him. I managed about half of it. It must have been watered down because we weren't that drunk. Just had to piss a lot and were full up! The only other thing I remember from that night, is one of the green coats coming over to our table at the end of the evening with an acoustic guitar. We sang loads of songs including Space Oddity about 3 times. Really good night though in the end. Nofuck (geddit!)

Back to Gary Numan gigs, the following year I went to the
2 Hammersmith Odeon shows in 1984. I'd decided to try
and dress up in this year's image. Unfortunately, it was the
year that Gary decided on blue hair and blue lipstick, white
face and white clothes. I was well into it even though
Numan was kind of on the slide by now. The first night, I
went by tube. It was pretty embarrassing really because as I
say, I decided to look the part like a lot of fans did back
then. I had on a white shirt, white face with blue lipstick
and blue hair. It was the eighties. It kinda looked passable
but I got some looks on the tube up to Hammersmith. On
the way back after a sweaty gig, I probably didn't look so
good. When I got in, I looked in the mirror and my face and
hair was just a big mass of blue and white. I looked more
like Coco the Clown rather than Gary Numan. Not good.
The next night, I decided to drive as I had passed my test
the day before. To this day, I don't know how I got there.
On the way, thick fog came down. I could only see about

ten feet in front of me. Eventually, "GARY NUMAN" in bold letters lit up on the outside of Hammersmith Odeon, appearing through the fog. I was really pissed off because the gig was about to start. I just parked the car to the side of the Broadway and ran in to the sounds of Berserker. I knew from the previous night that that was the first track of the night, so I didn't miss much. Phew. When I came out, my car was still there with no parking ticket. It would be ticketed and possibly towed away within minutes these days. More on Numan gigs later.

Gary Numan had started his own record label, and one of the bands on it was Hohokam who were one of the support acts for this tour. A band that I really liked. It was 1984 and I had passed my driving licence as just mentioned, but not really started to drink alcohol yet. This enabled me to follow them around when they played the following year. Mind you, by then I had found The Royal Hart, but decided to go and see them with a mate in London. I can't remember where, but they had got a new singer in by then.

I had also been going to a place called The Flag in Wembley. This was a venue that was annexed on from the Dog And Duck pub, and it's where there used to be Numan Discos as they were called back then, run by two guys called Pete and Frank. They also used to run the In The City magazine and promote alternative gigs.

I became one of the regulars I guess on the Numan scene. It was great going to Numan discos up and down the country, getting to know some of the regulars. It was another side of my personality away from The Royal Hart and looking back, I was also distancing myself from those terrible school days in various different ways. Somewhere where I could be completely different. I'd go to places like Kensington Market every now and again, and looked like a Numany goth I suppose. Great times. There were often bands playing at The Flag so I really enjoyed the whole scene. Having been to an all-boys school, it was also a good place to meet girls. Nothing serious but good fun. I wouldn't change a thing.

I remember once going to a Numan Disco in Swansea. Swansea! I went by coach with Caroline who sadly is no longer with us and Gloria. I think Karen was meant to come too. I was going out with her at the time but she couldn't make it. We got there early and met up with Debs, the organiser. It was in a bedsit I seem to remember as it was pretty cramped in there. The first person we met was a guy who was a cross dresser from Llanelli. Sounds like the start of a Limerick! I'd never met anyone like that and I was thinking "What have I let myself in for here." He seemed like a nice enough bloke though. I mean why wouldn't he be?

Debs was a bit flustered having never done this before. She was gutted because the pub had recently changed its name from The Park to Harry's Bar. There was a much-loved Tubeway Army single called Down In The Park which would've fitted perfectly – oh well.

I didn't know this at the time, but Debs informs me that there was a skinny Tarzonogram who turned up. She took the champagne off him and sent him packing. The night went well. We all had too much to drink and by the end, I remember a couple of us loosening those horrible polystyrene squares you used to get on the ceiling. It was good fun getting up on the chairs and poking them through until we got caught and chucked out. Bloody vandals, I know.

Now, I had never been to Swansea, let alone on a Saturday night. It must have been about 11pm to midnight, and the whole area was still packed with well-built rugby types, and that was just the women. I didn't want to get on the wrong side of any of them. We weren't ready to stop partying though, and someone said that they had a Gary

Numan compilation on cassette in their car parked up at the Kingsway multi-storey carpark.

"Let's go there and continue the disco!"

That seemed like a good idea, so we strolled over. A few of the pissed-up rugby types decided to follow us. Oh shit. This Numan fan got into his car, fired up the Quattro (OK, probably a battered old Vauxhall) and turned up the volume to max. It was great, Numan blaring out at 100 decibels with that echoey reverb from the indoor carpark. The rugby types and about a dozen of us all started dancing and carrying on like before. What a laugh. We must've been there for a good twenty minutes or so when the local constabulary decided to put a halt to things. We weren't doing any harm. Fascist bastards. Reluctantly we dispersed when the guy was told that he had to turn off the music. I think he turned it back on a couple of times and the police became a bit more hostile. It was a good night though. I have no idea where we stayed. Probably a cheap bed and breakfast and back on the coach into London the next day.

It was probably through talking to people at the Numan discos (disco is such a ridiculous word for describing them) when I found out where Gary Numan lived. I was still an obsessive fan, and as I lived near to where he was living, I felt compelled to visit his house. I'd heard about other fans going and having chats with him, and even being invited in on occasion. I'd made a few dummy runs as it was only about 8 miles away, and sure enough, the house name which I was told about (Lyndhurst if memory serves) had a Corvette Stingray outside with the number plate GN4. It had suddenly got real.

I'd decided to invite my new mate, Dagenham Dave for the actual visit on a date we'd agreed on.

The first time we tried, the gates were open, and we tentatively got out and rang the doorbell. An elderly gentleman answered and said that Gary wasn't in at the moment. I asked him if it was ok taking a couple of photographs of my car outside. He let me, so I took a couple of photos of my Mark 1 yellow Ford Capri, with black vinyl roof and the tackily scribed "NUMANOIDS" on the windscreen, a la Essex types with "Kevin And Tracy" or whatever they used to do. That reminds me, I remember going to the auto traders shop picking up the letters out of order so the guy at the counter didn't know what I was trying to spell. He kept asking me what I was spelling, and I told him that I wanted a couple of different options! It makes me laugh now thinking that Gary must've seen me driving around with that on the windscreen, as we lived so near each other. How embarrassing! I've still got the photos somewhere.

It was early one evening definitely towards the end of April 1985 when we tried again. I know the date for reasons that will become apparent later.

I drove up to the gates but this time they were closed. The good news though was that the lights were on and there was his Ferrari outside on the drive. Having being foiled a few times previously, we were determined to get in this time. We got out of the car, walked around to the back of the house, on to the busy A30 near Virginia Water lakes. We worked out where the correct house was, and attempted to climb over the fence and into the back garden. What were we thinking! It was that wiry green stuff that moves left and right and up and down as you're trying to climb it. I eventually managed it, my mate passed over my carrier bag of records, and now it was his turn. He got half way over then lost his balance. He did the old squashed knackers routine and shouted in pain. I was on the flooring nearly pissing myself with laughter. It was so funny. Why do we laugh when someone else hurts themselves?

He eventually got over and sorted himself out, and we took the short walk to the front of the house.

To the side of the house, neatly packed away like a full size premade airfix model, were the remains of his Cessna T210L light aircraft, that crash landed just off an A road near Southampton in early 1982. I'm not that much of a nerd. I had to look that up. It was just sitting there on a trailer. They had to do an emergency landing due to a fault. Gary was a passenger in his plane, but still got stick from the press for crash landing it.

"Ring the bell then" I said.

"I'm not ringing it" he replied.

Well, this went on for a couple of minutes, but there was no way I was going back now, so I just rang the bloody thing. I was so nervous just waiting. Nothing. I wasn't having it.

116

The lights were on. I rang it again. This time we heard something, the catch unlocked, and the door was kicked open from the inside like from a 70s cop show.

Time slowed down. There was Gary Numan with his hair stuck up and a massive shotgun pointing at my face. "WHAT THE FUCK DO YOU WANT?" he bellowed.

Well, after I'd stopped shitting my pants, I replied with what can only be described as the worst answer ever.

"We wanted to meet Gary Numan" I answered gingerly.

"I'M UPSTAIRS TRYING TO SCREW MY MRS AND YOU'RE BREAKING INTO MY PROPERTY JUST TO SEE 'GARY NUMAN!'"

The gun was still pointing directly at me. It's amazing what goes through your head in these situations. I remembered reading about this particular gun in Smash Hits or somewhere. It was the same kind of gun that was used by Clint Eastwood in the Dirty Harry films, and he'd bought one in America. I remember reading that they can kill someone from 2 miles away, and here it was pointing at my face. What a mess it would make.

After we apologised a few times and realising how foolish we'd been, he did calm down. He told us that he was particularly on edge at the moment, as he'd had death threats through the post to him and his parents. He mentioned that once, his dad actually found a bomb under his car. Crazy shit, so I get where he was coming from.

He explained that he didn't want his house to be turned into Fort Knox, and that he'd appreciate it if we passed on the message to other fans. If his gates were locked, nobody was welcome. If they were open, he would gladly come out and chat if he had the time. More than fair really. We told him that we would pass it on, but that we wouldn't visit again and we never did.

"Right, what's in your bag then?" he said.

"Oh, I brought along a couple of records that I hoped you would sign."

I passed over the carrier bag. The first record he pulled out was the new live album, "White Noise" which was released on 27th April 1985. That is how I can date the meeting.

"Where the fuck did you get this from?" he goes. His mood had now gone back to being angry from affable.

I told him that it had come out on Monday this week and that I'd got it from the record shop. He didn't believe me at first, but Dave backed me up and he realised that it must be true. He said normally he gets to see the proofs before albums are released, but after the tour he'd been away and he didn't have time. I think he thought that the release date was a few weeks later. He looked at the double album and opened it up looking at the photos.

"What do you think of the artwork?" he asked.

It was a gatefold double album. I told him that I thought the front cover was really good, the back cover was ok and that the middle was a bit blurry and disappointing to be honest. He agreed and probably wished he'd seen the proofs and changed it. He then signed it so I know that I have the first one signed.

He also asked why we made so much noise climbing over the fence. When I told him that Dave squashed his balls climbing over, he laughed as well. Not just me then.

He eventually ended up speaking to us for about an hour or so on his doorstep. His then girlfriend, Tracey made him a cup of tea half way through. He opened up when I asked him what it was like living on The Wentworth Estate. He said that he only uses a fraction of the rooms in his house, but he loves winding up his neighbour by making sure he says good morning or whatever when he sees him, because he was his old headmaster. He lives in a smaller house next door and always said that he'd amount to nothing.

"That's always enjoyable" he said and wasn't the answer that I was expecting.

When the conversation naturally stopped, he said,

"Right, you better be on your way now then."

We thanked him for taking the time to talk to us. It was great and we apologised again for startling him.

"How do we get out then?" I asked.

"You climbed in so you can fucking well climb out" he said with a smile this time.

We climbed over the front gates, waved goodbye and indeed did fuck off, pleased that we did finally manage to meet him.

Looking back, I can't believe we did that. A few years later I wouldn't dream of doing it but I'm kind of glad that we did. It makes for a good story if nothing else. It's funny, even with the gun pointing at my head, I was never scared.

I was more nervous about meeting him than getting my brains blown out.

Getting back to one of the Hohokam gigs, I went with the same Numan fan from Dagenham. Dagenham Dave. I must have met him up in London. I can't remember the venue but, on the internet, it says they played Dingwalls in Camden on February 16th 1987, which makes sense as it was very cold and on a Monday. I remember that I had to go to work the next day.

We had got to know them a little by now and naively, I was promised either somewhere to crash or a lift to Waterloo. I really can't remember, but needless to say, I got let down after the gig. The venue was not packed but we really enjoyed it. We'd had a couple of beers and my mate said he had to leave in order to get the last train back to Dagenham. So, there I was, a "wet behind the ears," 20-year-old, with enough money to either leave early and get home, buy one more beer, or a packet of fags out of the machine – fags it was. That was a mistake.

Reality struck when the gig was over. I was told that there was no room in the van after all   and I was stuck in Camden. Bollocks! I somehow managed to get to Green Park tube station but the tubes had now stopped. I got out in zero degrees temperature in just my t-shirt and leather motorbike jacket, and looked for somewhere to doss. This was well before phones and bank cards (for me at least) and I was skint by now anyway. I just had my travel card which I hoped I could still use first thing in the morning. I tried sleeping standing up in a phone box but it smelt of piss, and was just as cold. I kept getting people banging on it to use it too. What a nightmare.

I paced up and down to try and keep warm but I was tired, so just tried to kip behind one of the large columns by the steps of The Ritz. It kept the gusts of wind out at least. Old ladies would occasionally appear, decked out like a Christmas tree as the old song says, looking down on me. Literally and metaphorically.

I was probably only stuck out for about 4 hours before the tubes started again, but it was the longest night of my life. I can still feel the cold.

The good news was, I somehow managed to blag a new travel card from a very kind ticket lady, as she said mine wouldn't work anymore now. She must have taken pity on me seeing that I'd been caught out all night. The next bit is just weird. I managed to find my way back to Hounslow overground station, but I had to change to get back to Ashford. There was an outdoor shelter there with seats so I sat down feeling like shit. It was still bloody freezing and I was physically shaking from the cold. An elderly couple slowly walked over, and instead of ignoring me (normal train station behaviour) or at least asking how I was, they asked quizzically,

"Are you on heroin?"

I felt like just telling them to fuck off but I'd been brought up better than that.

"No, I said. I'm just really cold – please leave me alone."

They kept on,

"You look like you're coming off of heroin!"

I just ignored them, eventually got on the train, made my way home, got in to the relief of my mum and dad. I played it down like you do. They were more worried about me going to work. I told them that I would but I'm having a hot bath first, which I did. Ahh, that hot bath really was heaven.

Shit, look at the time, I got ready and drove to work. I was working as an input operator for DHL, and I was absolutely knackered. At least there was a free vending machine there. I said that I'm not feeling too good today. I must've had half a dozen chicken soups and done pretty much bugger all inputting! By midday, I'd had enough and went home without telling anyone, and slept right through to the following morning. I went back to work for the rest of the week as per normal, when on the Friday, the smarmy manager said,

"What are you still doing here?"

"What do you mean?" I said, "I work here."

"No, you don't. You were sacked three days ago."

No-one even had the decency to tell me. So, the moral to that story is, don't do all the things I did! At least I learnt a few lessons, albeit the hard way. Always make sure you can get home. Of course, it's easier nowadays with phones and a bit of money but I never did it again, even if it meant a few of us had to pay over the top for a cab or whatever.

Like I say, it was around this time that I started going to Kensington Market whenever I had enough money. It was a great place and much missed. If memory serves, I think it was two storeys high but it had a basement as well. It mainly sold clothes and accessories, but it also had a small record stall in there. It was great. It probably stunk of fags as you'd have to smoke whilst perusing everything. I had bleached hair, an earring, leather jacket with The Cure logo drawn in white paint on the back (actually, that came a bit later after I'd met Lisa), and my beloved Bowie trousers etc. We'd sometimes go to Carnaby Street too, but that was a bit more touristy and tackier. There was Reflections, a leather shop where Gary Numan got his stage gear right next to Ken Market. I went in once but just to look. I couldn't afford those prices. Opposite was Hyper Hyper where we would spot Sean (Tok from Tik And Tok) and SHOCK!

I once got stopped outside Virgin Radio with Karen (my then girlfriend). I was wearing my full-length leather trench coat that I got cheap off of my mate John. She had bleached back combed hair, almost a mohawk, and always looked good in her black gear. We had our photo taken and were asked a few questions. We ended up in No 1 magazine if anyone remembers that. The trench coat got nicked out of my car a few months later when we went out for a drink. I was gutted.

Another time, I was on my way home. I'd always get on the underground to Hatton Cross. As I got on, right near the back of the tube, I was daydreaming looking out of the window. It was much less busy down there in those days. I still had my bleached hair and was properly gothed up. I looked over and in the corner of my eye, I spotted someone. It was David Bowie. I started just staring like an idiot. It was only when the train started (and the doors were locked) that he gave me that enormous smile of his. As if to say,

"Yes, it is me but you can't get off and hassle me now!"

I read an article only a week or two later in a magazine. In it, they asked Bowie how he gets about town as he's so famous. He said that he took cabs mostly, but would also just take public transport too. People assume that it can't be me, so I mostly get away with it. Like I say, London was a lot quieter then.

Another time, I was coming back from somewhere late at night. The train was almost empty as it pulled in to Hatton Cross. As I got up, this guy strolled over from the next carriage. I hadn't noticed him before as he was behind me. He was fully suited and had jet black, slick backed hair. It was Nick Cave. I gestured to him to go out before me but he gestured back for me to go as I was first. Very cool.

More From The Hart

That's the funny thing about writing, you tend to go off on wild tangents, so it's nice to get back to The Royal Hart.

Another character was Andy. He would often get things wrong, especially after he'd had a few. I remember him once saying,

"He who laughs first, laughs last!"

That still tickles me to this day. Mind you, I'm guilty too. Once we were talking shit as per usual when someone asked,

"If you could be anyone, who would you like to be?"

For some unknown reason I replied,

"If I was a man, I'd like to be Billy Idol!"

Where did that come from? Another one that Andy got wrong was when we were talking about coming back for the evening session. Sunday's sessions were always the best. We'd get chucked out at 2pm. They moved it to 2:30pm and eventually 3pm. Well, my mate Ian said,

"I'll be back here dead on 7pm"

I said,

"In that case, I'll be here at 7 0' one"

Then Andy pipes up,

"I'm coming back at 7 0' ten then!"

It's not the funniest thing ever but it was really funny at the time and we always remember it.

I don't know what it is, but I don't like to be left out of anything. One evening, a few of us ended up in the lounge bar for some reason. There was a few of us in there. Someone had turned up with some amyl nitrate. It was known as the gay drug at the time but I won't go into that here. I was never really into drugs. I much preferred a pint, but having said that, I sometimes liked to try, just once. The drug, not the gay thing!

I went on asking for a hit and eventually I had my turn. Bloody hell, it was horrible. You get a really intense instant high that was too much for my little brain. I decided that I couldn't stay in the pub as people were staring (classic paranoia vibe) so I left my pint, which was not like me at all, and walked as far as the video shop at the other end of the high street to try and clear my head. "Steve The Video" ran it who was also a regular at the Hart. It was closed, but in the window, there were all these posters and cardboard point of sale stuff for a werewolf film or something. I was just getting my head together, when everything on the poster starting moving about and coming towards me. This was not good. I knew it was in my head but it still freaked me out (man). I walked back to the pub and eventually, the drug effect went away. I never tried that again, but it wouldn't be my last dabble with drugs. More of that later.

Another character that I remember was Brian. I think he was ex-army. He still had the dodgy 'tache. He managed to keep down a pretty good job in London. Something to do with printing, I think. He was stick thin, and at the beginning of a session, he would start off nice enough, but end up giving the new landlord, Jim, such grief. He must've barred him ten times or more, but the takings were probably well down so he kept being let back in. He just drank Guinness. Pints and pints and pints. I never saw him eat anything. I got there really early one Sunday. He asked me what I'd been up to and I told him that on the way here, I popped into my Nan's, and she wanted me to move her old washing machine from the kitchen to the drive, down the end of the garden but it was too heavy.

"Come on then, let's do it now"

It was only about half a mile away so we went round there, moved it and went straight back to the pub. It was so out of character because he was a nightmare when he'd had a few. He wouldn't even let me by him a pint. Such a shame that he was an alcoholic, because for that moment, he was as nice as pie.

The thing that made me laugh about Bwian as we called him as he couldn't pronounce his Rs, was that on occasion on a Saturday evening, he'd get out of his chair, pop outside to the call box, and call a cab. The first time he did this I asked him what he was doing as he'd always stay until the end. He probably told me to fuck off or something, and mind my own business. The cab driver came in and Brian would give him a tenner, and off he went without him. This went on for months and eventually I found out what was going on. The driver came in, got a tenner off of Bwian, went to the chippy to get cod and chips, and then drove it over to Brian's mum at the other end of Ashford and take it in for her. He would then pocket the change for doing it. Now that's class!

Brian died far too early and although he wasn't always easy to be around, he was a real character.

I remember a time when there was a little bit of trouble. It was over very quickly. The bloke got kicked out and we carried on drinking, playing pool and listening to the jukebox like normal. I thought nothing of it as you'd occasionally get a dickhead who turned up being a twat. Someone must have called the old bill though. When they turned up, they were being awkward. We tried to explain that the matter had been dealt with. They replied by informing us that there had been a complaint and we needed to give them our names and addresses, then we would have to leave. Well, we all ignored them at first but after a while, we realised that they weren't going to give up. I reluctantly gave them my details as did a few others. When it came to Ray, he blankly refused.

"Don't make this awkward for us or yourself sir. Just tell us your name and address, then you'll be free to go."

Ray wasn't having any of it. Just when they were going to cart him off, he said "OK then, I'll tell you."

"OK sir. What is your name?"

Ray slurred "Everyone calls me Mickey."

"Yes, but what is your actual name?" – "Mickey."

The policeman is getting fed up by now. "OK Mickey – second name?"

Ray replies incoherently.

"Sorry, I didn't get that."

Again, Ray says "Frugurshe"

"You'll have to write it down. I can't understand you."

"With a big grin, he writes "MOUSE"

The policemen says "Oh that's very original."

Ray then said that everyone calls him Mickey Mouse and he got nicked.

Someone said "Yeah, we always call Ray, Mickey Mouse!"

Just as he is getting carted off, I heard him say "Please radio ahead and inform Sgt Donaldson to get my usual room ready!"

He was obstinate but he was also a funny fucker was Ray!

As I write this, more memories keep popping into my head. There were a few of us on our way home from London. We had to change at Richmond in order to get the last train home. It must have been about 1990. We were all on the end platform awaiting the train. It's the train I now try and avoid because it has all the pissheads on it who want to talk to you because they're pissed. Well, on this occasion, I was that annoying person. I'm not sure how it started but I had The Soup Dragons song in my head. You remember. "I'm free, to do what I want, any old time" A superior cover of The Rolling Stones classic in my opinion.

It kept going over and over in my head, and for that matter, outside of my head too.

 What with the natural reverb of the enclosed part of the outside station, to my ears it didn't sound too bad so I kept singing it. Very loudly.

"I'M FREE, TO DO WHAT I WANT, ANY OLD TIME."

 I was getting a reaction now, so, with the aid of an evening's worth of lager down my neck, I proceeded to walk up and down the platform singing and conducting my audience and going up to people. Ok, mainly young women, and the dangly bit on my leather jacket became the fake microphone. I'd pass it over, and most would start singing into my leather jacket. Ha ha. By the time the train came, I got pretty much the whole platform singing it.

Great fun. I really should've been on the stage. I've

basically wasted my life……………….

Three Go Mad In Sunbury

It was some time in 1988 that myself, Ade and another mate, Jon who lived near the Royal Hart, all decided to rent a house for a year in nearby Sunbury. Peregrine Road to be precise.

Due to this, The Royal Hart took a bit of a back seat, and we frequented a pub called The Jolly Gardener. It's called The Grizzly Bear now. It was a proper local pub for local people. We got to know some of the regulars. I'd also taken over from Ade where he worked, as a delivery driver and warehouseman for a small damp proofing company in Staines. The job entailed delivering bags of render and timber on site for the more specialised workmen. It was a messy job, clearing up all the rubble and stuff but it got me as fit as I'd ever been. I've never been naturally fit, but I was whilst doing that job. It lasted about a year before I'd had enough and left to be a courier which is what I do to this day.

I also met my future wife, Lisa, whilst living in Peregrine Road. It was obviously meant to be as we kept bumping in to each other through mutual friends. Eventually, we got set up and agreed to start seeing each other. The rest as they say is history.

As I write this, we have been together for nearly 36 years and we just get on. Well, mostly.

I think we were just meant to be.

Back to Peregrine Road. It was good fun a lot of the time. Ade had now joined Kabuki Smiles. He was the singer and they mostly did covers of The Clash, Eddie Cochran, U2 and stuff like that. It was great seeing them play. Mostly in a pub called The Compasses in Egham but more on that later.

We were really bad at doing chores around the house. Imagine The Young Ones mixed in with a bit of Withnail And I and you'll get the idea. Toast toppers was the food of kings. Disgusting baby food but it's all we could afford, if we wanted to go down the pub most nights. I remember once that we decided to cut the grass out the front. We'd left it for months and it was about a foot high. All the neighbours came out and started clapping ironically. Very embarrassing but funny.

Adrian was interesting to live with. He was a decent bloke but he couldn't handle his booze, so it could be stressful at times. There was an incident where we invited back a few of the regulars. I had to go to work early the next morning and I was really tired, so I said I was going to bed. Ade didn't like this and followed me up the stairs hurling abuse. I had a go back at him which I didn't normally do. Normally, anything for a quiet life. Well, one thing led to another and we were in each other's faces. One of the blokes from the pub ran up and separated us. The bullying from my schooldays came flooding back and he was trying to make me look foolish in front of everyone. Like I say, I was tired. The guy who separated us said,

"You both calmed down now?"

I said "Yes, I'm fine."

When he let go of me, with all my might I smacked Ade a left hook in to his face. I can't remember ever hitting anyone before that really. He left the room, everyone left the house. and I barricaded myself in for the night in case he seeked revenge! Sorry Ade if you're reading this!

I went to work the next day and got back early. I hated hitting someone and it was stressing me out. I was dreading Ade coming back. He eventually bowled in with the biggest black eye. He looked at me, I looked at him and we both just started laughing. I think he knew he'd been a bit of a tit. He said,

"I didn't think you would hit me with my glasses on."

I was so wound up that I hadn't even noticed that he was wearing glasses. I must have lumped him just underneath them. I think he actually respected me more after that cause it bloody hurt. There were some good times and bad. Ade could make an average night into the best night ever, but he could also ruin a perfectly good evening by doing something silly. There was a time when he got in from the pub, probably having not eaten all day, cooked himself a full english breakfast at about 11 at night. I came down in the night because the light was still on in the kitchen. There he was lying face up on the kitchen floor, eggs, bacon, mushrooms, beans etc on a plate on his lap, half a mug of tea still in his left hand turned cold, and a fag burnt down to the filter in his gob. I'd never seen anything like it. It was so funny. I think I took a photo but I must've given it to him.

We had found out about this goth nightclub in London. Doing some research, I think it was called The Catacombs in Manor House, North London. We'd decided that we would go. It must've been late 80s. I used to dress a bit gothic and so did Ade actually although that was more down to his stage look. He was more into Dead Or Alive, King and stuff like that, but we were both well up for it. It was a Friday afternoon so we got ready, and somehow Jon or Ade got hold of some ecstasy tablets. We'd heard that they take ages to work, so we had them just as we left. I was going to drive to Hatton Cross and Jon would drive my car back as he wasn't going.

All was well for about ten minutes, until I started giggling at things that weren't particularly funny. Ade and Jon said that I'd better pull over and let Jon drive the rest of the way. I remember saying that I was fine, but about 5 minutes later, I took the decision to do just that. I'm not completely stupid! We got to Hatton Cross and managed to get our tickets for the tube. The goth look tended to get a few stares at the best of times. On a very bright Friday afternoon, even more so. It was now about 5pm, and the train was mainly full of suited businessmen, as we made our way into central London. I remember sitting on one side, and Ade was opposite and a little way down the carriage as the train was pretty full.

I was just trying to keep my shit together now as the ecstasy tab was well and truly kicking in. It was a nice fuzzy feeling and I'm sure I had a fixed grin. Everyone normally looks really pissed off on tube trains, even on a Friday evening, so I just kept my head down. We were now in West London, but Manor House was near Cockfosters at the end of the line, and it was a continuous journey the whole way. We got through the West End and kept going. It was a long journey, both literally and in our heads. I was bored looking down and the blood was rushing to my head, so I decided to brave it and look up. I could see Adrian's shoulders bobbing up and down and his face was bright red and his eyes were streaming. He was trying so hard to keep it together but something had tickled him. He kept nodding at me to look at someone. I didn't understand. Then he came over trying not to fall over as the train was still moving, and tried whispering, but the tube train was too noisy to hear anything.

The suited businessmen were starting to ruffle their broadsheets by now pretending not to notice anything. It was all too much for Ade. When the train stopped, he got up again, started laughing and shouted at the top of his voice,

"PHIL COOL – IT'S PHIL COOL!"

and he was pointing at this poor, bemused person who looked nothing like Phil bloody Cool. We used to watch Phil Cool videos in the house and his stand up was a favourite of ours. This bloke however, definitely was not

Phil Cool. The whole carriage was now staring at these 2 goth twats who not only broke the 4th wall, but were laughing so hard, that it became infectious and people were smiling at us. Well, some were and some gave us daggers but either way, it is not traditionally how goths are supposed to act. You are supposed to be moaning about everything, smell of petunia oil, and talk about conspiracy theories whilst wearing leathers, that had been run over loads of times in the road to give them that authentic, worn in look.

It was time to bail out a few stops early. There's no way we could stay in there any longer.

We got out still laughing at our behaviour, when Ade said he needed to sort himself out and get some chips or something. We were on a busy London high street when sure enough, we found a chippy. I wasn't hungry at all so I waited by the door. I'll never forget what happened next. Maybe you had to be there but it was so unintentionally funny. Maybe it was the timing.

The Greek guy behind the counter said,

"Yes please?"

Ade mustered up as much soberness as he could find (which wasn't much) and finally slurred out the words,

"Fishhnnnchiiippsssss!"

Not what type of fish, not even a please at the end of it just "Fishhnnnchiiippsssss!" It was so funny. The guy just looked at him bemused. Adrian managed to get in to his pocket underneath his full-length trench coat, and chuck about five pounds of shrapnel on to the counter, still laughing his head off, coins spinning around, 10ps spilling to the floor, even 2 and 5 pence pieces flying about. He realised his mistake and just walked out sans fish or indeed chips.

"Ade, you need to sober up a bit before talking to anyone" I said.

149

It was agreed so we took a long walk to the Manor House pub. Things had got better now and once we got there, we managed a beer or two and went in.

All I remember of the evening, were these gorgeous goth girls doing this dance where they just walked forwards and backwards in time to The Sisters Of Mercy or something. I think we had a good night though and as we were leaving, Ade was chatting up this really over the top goth girl. Think Siouxsie times 3. Not looks wise or anything, just how she appeared. Head to toe in various forms of black material and loads of silver jewellery; you get the idea. He seemed to be doing quite well until she asked him what his favourite song was. Now, I'm guessing that he's gonna think on his feet and lie. Maybe say Bella Lugosi's Dead by Bauhaus, something from the Sisters Of Mercy or The Mission. I mean, he did know those bands. Maybe even The Cure or Siouxsie. No, he decided that this goth girl would like him to say Cruel To Be Kind by Nick Lowe! I mean, I love a bit of Nick Lowe and that is probably one of his best tracks, but don't say that! Why did he say that? I can still see her in my mind's eye laughing and trying to get away. He was making things worse by trying to explain his decision. I mean The Sisters did do some weird covers admittedly but don't say that!

We soon made our way home - on our own.

On a few occasions, well before we moved in, we would randomly take a day off sick. These would be "planned" on the way back from the Hart after 4 or 5 pints on a whim the night before. I had a shitty job working as an import/ export clerk and I hated it. It was a small office and everyone bitched about someone as soon as they left the room. Horrible people. Due to this, I didn't need much persuasion to take a sickie, so in the morning, I'd pretend to go to work (to fool my parents) and then go around the corner and meet up with Ade. Due to his inheritance, he had a decent motor for an 18 or 19 year old. A brand-new silver

Ford Escort Mark 3. He'd already sold his VW Campervan before. He'd forgotten that there was still sick in the kitchenette bit where he threw up a few days previous – yuck!

We would normally go to places like Hayling Island or Hastings. I don't know why. Actually, I've just remembered something apropos to nothing, but it was funny. As I said previously, Ade was from Birmingham and now and again we'd go up and visit his old mates in a place called Streetly. It was always a good weekend away. This is obviously well before phones and internet. We were on our way back on a cold winter's evening. It was Sunday and we weren't looking forward to work the next day. Now Ade had done this journey a dozen times or more, but I think he wanted to go back via the scenic route. I don't know why as it was pitch black by now. I could see that he was getting agitated. The radio was turned off (for extra concentration) and he tried his best to get us back on track.

We were in the middle of nowhere. I kid you not, we'd been driving for another half an hour after this, when I noticed something that we'd passed an hour ago. That was it.

"AAAARRRGGGHHHH!!!!!!!" Adrian had now lost the plot.

"I'VE HAD ENOUGH OF THIS!" and slams on the brakes and punches the steering wheel. We just sat there in silence. It was probably only a few seconds but it felt like minutes. There was tension in the air and he was about to snap.

He decided to take his mind off things by turning on the radio. Imagine the dark, quiet tension and frustration. What came on the radio was the funniest thing. Talk about wrong song for how we were feeling. Do The Hucklebuck by Coast To Coast. It's such a ridiculously happy, cheerful and cheesy song. If you are lucky enough to not know it, do yourself a favour and look it up quickly on your phone. We were in silence for about 3 seconds and then we just couldn't stop laughing. Tears rolling down our eyes. It was such a change of tone but just what we needed. We were pissing ourselves laughing until the song finished, but it seemed to do the trick. We made our way straight home after that.

Now, where was I? Oh yes, this time, myself, Ade and Jon all went to Hayling Island. It was a long time ago and I had to be reminded some of this by Jon. I'm pretty sure that we stayed overnight on this occasion. I imagine we found a cafe first. Always loved a seedy coastal cafe to have some greased tea as Morrissey so eloquently put it. We then went looking for pubs. By the afternoon, someone decided that we should play a game. Not fatty's game! See who could steal the best thing from the pub. I don't think I wanted any part in it really so I stole a beermat. Actually, thinking about it. I think I stole a Style Council single from the DJ too because I've still got it. Jon managed to sneak out a heavy ashtray. Adrian always had to go one better. He got a bloody fire extinguisher!

After some more pubs it was decided that we should go to the beach. We always seemed to go out of season but I think we bumped into some people who were messing around making a fire on the sand. It was never gonna get out of control as we had our very own fire extinguisher. Jon got off with one of the girls. Ade kindly referred to her as a beached whale. We decided to save Jon by running over, picking him up, sticking him in the boot and driving off! It would've been good had it not been for the fact that Jon needed to go back for his coat which was still lying on her. Bollocks. It was all just a bit of fun I suppose.

There was another time that just myself and Ade went, probably pulling a sickie again. We met these 2 girls in the pub. After a while we asked them what they were up to. They said to follow them as they were going back to theirs. Seemed like a good idea. I reckon they had cold feet as they whizzed around corners that they knew, as they were local. Adrian's rallying skills weren't quite up to it and we ended up in a ditch. I think the RAC bailed us out. I really can't remember.

He should've let me drive. After I passed my test, me and a workmate called Brian used to go off for a drive on a Saturday. It always seemed to be icy or snowy and we found this multi-story car park in Guildford. You could go in without paying in those days. We would get to the top level and slide about on the snow or ice. It was great fun but also good practice. We got really good at controlled skidding and sliding about. I lost touch with Brian after we went out for an evening drive in his new car. It was an old Triumph Herald. There was a humpback bridge ahead.

I remember saying, "Floor it!"

He didn't so I gave him a load of grief. Peer pressure is a terrible thing. He turned around and renegotiated the bridge at full pelt. It was great, we were giggling as we hit the air. Then his face dropped as the undercarriage collapsed on re-entry. He called out his dad. I got the blame and we lost touch after that. It was well worth it though. Never felt so good to be alive!

I think I only took acid or ecstasy 3 times. I didn't even know what the difference was. As I say, it wasn't what I was in to. It just seems that every time we took it – something memorable happened. I suppose it would. I'm not sure why, but we all took a tab of something. Ade had a bad trip and I seem to remember him climbing on top of a bus shelter and shouting out random things. We decided it would be safer to get back and stay indoors while the effects wore off. I used to smoke back then, just roll ups or B&H. I went upstairs to have a lie down. There were a few people downstairs milling about. They kept hearing this "schoom" noise every now and again, and then it would go. After about half an hour, someone came upstairs and said,

"What are you doing?"

"Schoom" I replied as I was lying on my bed in the dark waving my fag about. Apparently, I could see the light trail really clearly. You know, like in the Kate Bush Wuthering Heights video "Schoom!"

I wasn't feeling quite so clever the next day, but I really needed to go to the bank in Staines for some reason. It was a hot day and the after effects were kicking in. I think I may have passed out. A few people helped me up and I just about got myself sorted out. I got back and into bed. Jon said he came in later and I looked like shit. I think the bed did too if you get what I mean. No more tabs for me after that.

Jon had his moments too. He came in my room off his head one evening. He'd been sniffing deodorant spray. Silly sod. Mind you, he smelt great! Let this be a warning kids.

Ade had started seeing this girl, Eve. She was really nice and we all got on well on the few nights that we'd had out. We went to a place called The Cider House in Winkfield. Right next to where Legoland is now. It's long gone. They used to sell really strong cider. One was called GBH. There was another called depth charge which had a glass of something else in it. A bit like those revolting Jager bombs. Every time we went, someone threw up. Not us, other punters. The bar area had an internal roof which was thatched like the outside. I remember picking Eve up once, she was only little, and pinning her to the internal roof. She blurted out,

"You've thatched me!"

I don't know why but it amused us, but it just did.

We all got to know each other a bit better so the four of us decided to go camping, as we'd never been before. Well, I hadn't anyway. Adrian found this camp site near Oxford, so off we went one Saturday just for one night. Once we got there, we made our way to the site. All I remember is pitching up this little tent that we were all supposed to share. It gets a bit fuzzy after that, but we just started tucking in to the cans of lager, when Adrian and Eve had this big fight. Awkward. I think we all just crashed and hoped things would be better in the morning. I remember waking up with a feeling that my Saturday night had been ruined. Ade started making a fire for breakfast. There was an undercurrent of a bad atmosphere, so I did something that I hadn't done before or since. I said,

"Well sod it, I'm having a beer."

I cracked open a lager at about 8 in the morning. We only had a couple of tins the night before and had loads left. This probably wasn't a good idea as Adrian followed and opened one of his.

"Fuck it."

You don't need many beers before you start feeling a bit tipsy in the morning, so after we had breakfast washed down with a few tins of cheap lager, it was decided that Eve would drive us all in to Oxford itself. We drove for a while when we saw the Oxford University. Myself and Ade wanted to explore, so we asked the girls to wait while we went in. It was definitely out of term but the gates were open. We just walked in. The first thing we did was go into the chemistry classroom. It was empty so we sat down at the desk pretending to be Scumbag College or something when we got a shock. An old guy in white overalls wandered in busily preparing something.

"Good morning" he said as he gestured towards us.

"Er, good morning, Sir" we replied.

He didn't ask who we were or anything so we slowly just walked out laughing. Time to explore some more. We found the student accommodation block. It was totally empty but we couldn't get in anywhere. One thing we noticed, was that on each floor, there was an outside fridge. We had a look in them but there was nothing much inside. Adrian had this brilliant idea. Remember, we'd had a few. There were 3 floors. We could unplug and move each fridge on to a different floor. That would really confuse them when they come back for the new term. We struggled lifting these bloody heavy fridges giggling away as we were doing so. Eventually, job done. Each fridge was now on a different floor and nobody saw us. This would've been a brilliant wheeze as Oxbridge types would probably say, except, that it was the end of term and these students had probably left now. Also, it then dawned on us that we could have just moved the contents of each fridge, not the whole bloody thing. Oh well, it made us laugh anyway. I bet security is better these days. We came home after that. Ade fell asleep in the car; I got dropped off at the pub, and he came in about 2 hours later with the right hump saying that I should've woken him up. We had a good night anyway telling anyone that would listen about our Oxford University exploits.

When Ade asked myself and Jon to carry on and rent the house for another year, we bailed out. I couldn't have handled another year. We went back to our parent's houses. Ade got a bit funny about that as he didn't want to go back home. It was ok though. He eventually found a little flat in Ashford and we remained friends for a bit longer, but we did lose touch over time. He did come and visit one night about 20 years later which was great for reminiscing about the good old days.

The Booze Cruise To France

Ray, the guy who fell asleep into his omelette, and on another occasion got carted off to the police cells, suggested that myself and another mate of mine, Mark, drive over to France for a booze cruise. The idea being that we drive to Dover, and get a ferry over to Calais. Whilst we were there, we would stay overnight for a change of scenery. It seemed like a good idea so we agreed. He said he'd get his sister's boyfriend to come along as driver and general dogsbody. We would leave on a Saturday morning, stay overnight, and then come back on the Sunday evening. What a laugh it was.

Back then, I kind of lived day to day. I was down the pub on this particular Friday night, and was reminded that we were going to France the next morning. I was still living at home, and had previously mentioned to my parents, that I might be going to France for the weekend but it wasn't definite.

Ray said that it was now definitely on, so I gave him my address, and actually got a bit excited, and drank far too much on the night before. By the end of the evening and after a few neat JDs for the road, he said,

"I'll be outside yours at about 9am. You'll be ready, won't you?"

"Yeah yeah, of course – see you tomorrow" I nonchalantly replied.

Well, I was out for the count. The next thing I know, the others are at the door first thing and I have the worst hangover ever. I shouted down that I wasn't going. My dad came up and said that I'd better get up, and quick. He said that I couldn't let people down like this at the last minute. I sat up and tried to get my head straight. I was fucked but guess he was right. I chucked some clothes on, packed a carrier bag of clean clothes for the next day, and trundled off downstairs. They were laughing because I looked rough as fuck. Ray had turned up in his Luton van.

"There's no more room in the front, you'll have to get in the back."

Great, that should be good for my hangover I was thinking.

"Have you got everything?"

"Yeah, let's go" I managed to grunt in reply.

Except, I didn't have everything. In fact, it could be said that the one thing I definitely needed, I did not have – my passport!

They gave me ten tons of grief for not having a passport, but Ray said that we could stop at Staines post office on the way and get a temporary one. If you can't get one, I'll drop you off back home. God, I hope I can't get one I was thinking. It was very difficult to get comfy in the back of that bloody Luton. You couldn't sit down and if you stood up, you'd fly around like a cat in a tumble dryer. Not that I've ever put a cat in a tumble dryer. I rather like cats – in fact, I like most animals, but I imagine a cat in a tumble dryer, would've resembled my good self in this circumstance. The lorry eventually stopped, I jumped out and threw up in the middle of Staines hight street on a busy Saturday morning. My head was pounding. I just wanted my bed.

To cut a long story short, I got a passport – you could do that back then, and off we went to Dover – oh great.

The next thing I remember is getting on board the ferry. The first port of call was the bar. Well, that was the last place I wanted to be. Myself and Mark found a gift shop and for reasons which I still can't explain, we each bought a glove puppet. I know. Mine was a white rabbit and I think I'd always wanted a puppet as a kid. We started re-enacting a puppet show, sliding them down the banisters and generally being rather silly. My hangover was subsiding and I think I was still a bit pissed from the night before. Mark said,

"Are you ready for a beer now, Span?"

I think it was a good couple of hours ferry ride, so reluctantly I said OK. I nursed one pint until we got there. By now the others had had a few and I was feeling much better. We were in France and I think we were all up for having a good laugh.

The next thing I remember is Ray getting Steve to drive us to this area, where he said it would be good for finding a place to stay. Seeing as Ray had been many times before through his work, driving artics about, and the fact that he was a good bit older, we let him take charge. We went into this establishment. Ray seemed to know the owner, and we got the drinks in.

"This will be a good place to stay" suggested Ray.

Well, it wasn't long before myself and Mark thought it was pretty ropey in there, and probably a knocking shop. You don't hear that expression anymore, do you? Mark was adamant that we should find somewhere else to stay and I backed him up. Ray reluctantly agreed and said he knew another place which was more of a traditional hotel.

We found this other place, and actually, it looked great. A nice big "chain" type of hotel with a decent bar area, and we soon got checked in to our individual rooms. Mark warned me not to touch the mini bar as it'll be ridiculously expensive. With that in mind, we sorted ourselves out and met in the generous bar downstairs. We could relax now and get a few beers in. After a while I was well away and so was Mark. I think Steve buggered off somewhere else and to Mark and my amazement, Ray went up to his room at about 9pm. We all liked a beer but Ray really liked a beer if you know what I mean, so it was a bit weird, especially as we were only staying one night.

Oh well, we carried on and had a few more. At one point, I remember Mark saying that he had to go to the loo. I would normally wait to save our seat, but I really needed to go too, so after a short while I decided to go. You had to walk behind the bar itself. It was quite modern. All lit up with glass and mirrors. Very 80s. Just as I was walking around the back, admittedly checking out the two sexy French barmaids, Mark was coming out of the toilets on the other side, behind the glass panelling which partitioned the bar area. Mark saw me looking at the 2 girls, and did his best Rik Mayall impression, thrusting himself backwards and forwards doing the finger in the hole motion that Rik used to do. I was laughing at Mark which made him do it even more. It was kind of risky as it was only a glass bar and they might have turned around at any second. As they didn't, he got more into it, thrusting and gurning away. I was laughing uncontrollably now, because what he hadn't noticed, were 2 very elderly French looking guests walking very slowly behind him, giving him one of those "looks" – you know the ones. The looks that you give when not only are you disgusted with what you are seeing, but you don't really understand it either.

Mark must have seen me catch their eye. He turned around and his face went from laughing and doing Rik, to just having all the confidence drained out of him. The humiliation, embarrassment and just mortification was too much. It made it all the funnier to me – brilliant.

The next morning, we had a big day ahead of us. This was our main day and we were gonna make the most of it. I got up and saw a bleary-eyed Ray look over from his room and put his finger to his mouth to shush me. What I saw next was genius. Wrong, but genius all the same. He had drunk all the contents of his mini bar the night before!

It was not an insignificant amount in there either. As I recall, there was half a bottle of champagne, some lagers, ciders, a few miniatures and mixers. It was now completely empty bar the odd mixer. He was now following the maid about surreptitiously, and was awaiting his opportunity to pounce. Sure enough, she nipped out of the room that she was cleaning. Ray ran in, emptied the bar and replaced every item into his own mini bar. I reckon that was his plan all along, hence leaving us early the night before. Dodgy bastard!

Of course, you can't do that nowadays as I believe the drinks are now connected to a computer system, using infrared technology, so they know when you've taken one and it's charged to your bill automatically. He told us to get ready as we're checking out. I really thought he wouldn't get away with it as the receptionist was going through everything, but he bloody well did. I'd love to have seen the poor unsuspecting soul who got charged for it. That would've been an interesting conversation. He was clever Ray, but morally reprehensible at times.

We weren't sure what to do next. I guess we got some breakfast somewhere and headed for the nearest bar. I don't remember much but, we didn't like where we were and it was freezing outside, so we ended up in this massive snooker hall. We all loved a bit of pool down the pub, and the few times that I'd played snooker, I really enjoyed it. It's much harder but more rewarding when you stroke in a long red or whatever. It didn't take long before we were topping up from the night before and having a few frames of snooker. We weren't planning on staying long but it was now snowing outside.

I think Ray was getting itchy feet after a while, so in his best pigeon French, he asked a group of locals if there were any good bars nearby. One of them looked like an even more thuggish Alexei Sayle. Not that Alexei Sayle is thuggish, he just looks it. They all seemed a bit worse for wear as we probably did to be honest. What happened next was just so random and a real mood killer. The Alexei Sayle like character got out some porn photos. We just thought it was going to be the usual titillation type thing that you'd occasionally see. Well, I won't go into details, but the first photo was of a paedophilic nature. I won't repeat here what it was, but it was just wrong. He of course found it very amusing, especially with our reaction. I kind of wish we'd just piled in but we wouldn't have stood a chance. Fair play to Ray. He just said,

"We don't like that sort of thing where we're from."

There was a bit of abuse and we just walked out. I was expecting a dig in the back on the way out, but thankfully nothing happened.

We went for a walk to clear the air. I imagine that we hit a couple of bars and then Ray got Steve to drive us to the hypermarket to stock up on booze and fags. There's a bit of a theme here isn't there. It's funny, I had such a good time in those days, but I'm glad I don't drink anywhere near as much now. Maybe I've just had my fill. Don't get me wrong, I still have my moments but I save drinking mainly for gigs and footy these days.

The next bit is funny. We must have been well oiled because we were having shopping trolley races around the hypermarket. I was whizzing Ray around and I remember him grabbing a packet of ham slices off the shelf, which he proceeded to open, and shove down his gullet. Having been told off by security a couple of times, we just filled up the trollies with lager and went to pay. Ray was just in front of me at the till, when the cashier added up the bill and included the empty packet of ham in the trolley. Straight faced, Ray said that it wasn't his. She said that she saw him eating it, but no, Ray wasn't having any of it.

"I'm not paying for something I've not had" Ray said, so once again, security was called. I said,

"Ray, come on mate, just pay for it. It's all over your mush!"

He was so bloody stubborn though, and it was only when myself and Mark tried to pay for it, that he backed down. We just wanted to get on with things. It was funny though. He was stubbornly exclaiming his innocence with remnants of ham all over his teeth and mouth.

By now it was getting late, and Mark was getting worried that we wouldn't make the ferry in time, and he seemed to sober up. I didn't give a shit. We had The Stranglers blaring out full blast, Rattus Norvegicus, and myself and Ray were singing along as loud as we could with the windows down. Mark was also a massive fan of The Stranglers, but he just wanted to get back now.

I was enjoying myself. Ray kept giving wrong directions and Mark (probably quite rightly) felt that he was stalling in order for us to spend another night over there. Mark wasn't having any of it and we made it to the ferry in the nick of time. It was a weird weekend, and one that myself and Mark will never forget. Ray, in a similar way to Adrian could make an average day or evening turn into one of the best days ever, but also vice versa. Ray, like Brian is no longer with us. Another reason why I'm glad I don't drink like I used to. RIP Ray and Brian.

Boring Wednesdays

Sometimes you'd find yourself down The Royal Hart on a wet and boring Wednesday evening, and it just wasn't happening. Not enough people came out or whatever. I remember a mate of mine; John had just got back from living in California for about a year or so, and he came down expecting a brilliant night. I think he was told to leave by Jim the landlord because he had called him some names on the phone when he was in L.A. It's a long story. There was me, John, Richard and Steve. Steve said,

"Why don't we go down the Links for a change. I'll drive as I've not had a drink yet."

It seemed like a good idea and it was only a few minutes away by car. On the way, John and Richard sparked up this almighty spliff. I was never one for a puff but when in

Rome. Jesus, this was some strong shit. All the windows were done up and you could hardly see in there. Steve told us that he needed petrol for the morning so he pulled into the garage opposite the pub. We were still puffing away when he came back and very kindly gave us all a Turkish Delight. I had opened the window by now but it looked like the car was on fire due to the amount of smoke, so I wound it up again. We were in a petrol garage after all. It was so funny. Steve started munching on his Turkish delight as we all were. He then said,

"I don't know why I bought these really. I fucking hate Turkish Delight."

Rich says "Me too" then John in the back says,

"Me too" and then I say,

"Actually, I don't like them either!"

We all start laughing and John goes to throw his bar out of the window and it went splat! He didn't realise that I'd wound the window back up. It was so funny. I mean, even

if we hadn't been smoking, it would've still made us laugh,

but the fact that we had, just made it funnier. We ended up

having a really good night after that. For a Wednesday.

Kabuki Smiles

As previously mentioned, Ade had joined this college band, Kabuki Smiles as lead singer. It was mainly a covers band although they did write a couple of decent tracks towards the end.

There was Phil on drums. You had Dave on bass and Ian, his brother, on lead guitar. Ade was on vocals. Ade used to like me to come along and watch them rehearse every Tuesday in Phil's dad's warehouse. I enjoyed it at first but it was a bit boring after a while, but I had nothing better to do back then and it kept me out of the pub. I'm trying to remember what else they played. Garageland and I Fought The Law by The Clash, C'mon Everybody, a Housemartins instrumental, Boys Don't Cry, Love Me Do, Hi Ho Silver Lining, When Will I Be Famous by Bros. Not really, just seeing if you're paying attention! I think they did In God's

Country and New Year's Day too. The Joshua Tree was massive at the time. That kind of stuff anyway. Phil's older brother Steve was also in a band called Intimate Strangers, who did a different yet similar set. A few punk tracks and pre Britpop type stuff. It was great though. In fact, their drummer, Smiler, or Steve as I knew him back then, went on to play with the likes of Robbie Williams, Joe Strummer, From The Jam and the last time I saw him, he was playing in The Alarm. A great drummer. There was a pub in Egham called The Compasses. It's still there actually although it's recently closed. Kabuki Smiles and Intimate Strangers used to take it in turns to play there. It seemed like every other week, and they would both have a good following from the college students mainly.

We used to get pretty pissed and everyone was always up for a good night. I reckon it held a about a hundred people. One night, Russ Abbot turned up to watch his boy playing in the support band. Abbot was quite well known at the time and he turned up slightly in disguise wearing a cloth cap. Well, I wasn't having any of that. I half drunkenly went up to him, and attempted to do the inebriated Scottish character that he always seemed to be doing on his TV show. I got no reaction. Nothing! The equivalent of leaving me hanging, he just ignored me. I don't blame him really, although I did at the time. Oh well, another "Spanner" moment.

Quite quickly Kabuki got better. They wore more extravagant stage clothes, and managed to get a few London gigs. The Red Lion in Brentford, which is now a Tesco's was one of them.

They also played The Rock Garden in Covent Garden. Not many turned up for that one. Probably mid-week but there was a brilliant band on after them. I wish I knew who they were. There was a 50s rock'n'roll looking singer, a long-haired heavy metal guitarist, a new romantic type on synths, and there was about 7 of them on stage. They all looked different. It was brilliant.

The only other gig in London that I can remember, is The Greyhound in Hammersmith which I knew quite well because my old girlfriend, Karen, lived really nearby and we'd often go there. I was with Kabuki when they were trying to get this support slot. I don't think the guvnor wanted cover bands, but when they told him that I was their roadie, and I'd roadie for the headline band as well for just £20, it seemed to seal it.

Now, I've never done anything to do with being a roadie. I can tie up my shoelaces, that's about it. I was a bit worried but the band said that I'll be fine – just wing it. Well, the day came. I helped Kabuki set up their stuff, but they all knew what they were doing so I kept it simple. They played their set – all was good.

The next thing I know, this intimidating long haired singer in the main band, beckoned me over and said,

"After the first number, I always seem to break a guitar string. That's ok, just bring on the white Fender or (whatever it was), take this and restring it while I'm playing. I won't need it back for another 3 or 4 songs.

Oh shit, what do I do? I'm thinking to myself.

"Yes, no probs." I badly lied. He looked at me and said,

"You can string a guitar and tune it can't you?"

"Of Course," I lied again.

He gave me one of those looks. He knew I was bullshitting I think but he had no other option. I was praying that his guitar strings would hold up, but oh no, that would be too easy, wouldn't it?

Padink – there goes one. Padink – fuck me, another. I took his guitar at the end of the song and exchanged it for the white one as requested. He carried on playing, and every now and again in between songs he was berating me in the wings for not restringing it. It was awful. I probably went red and he eventually just told me to fuck off. So, I did. Downed a couple of quick pints. The band (Kabuki) were all taking the piss out of me. Bastards.

This band really thought they were something though. Poodle permed nonsense if I remember. They had a track called "Money" or something. Not a cover of Pink Floyd or The Beatles/ Flying Lizards track. I think it was one of their own. They obviously thought it was this masterpiece, as towards the end of the track, this netting came away, you know, the ones that normally prop up balloons, and down came all these photocopied 5 and ten pound notes. I'm pretty sure that you're not supposed to do that. And here's why. I picked up a bundle, scrunched them up to make the notes look old, and in the dimly lit bar area, I managed to buy 2 rounds of beers in the next half an hour!

When the band finished, I felt bad. Not about getting the free beer, but nearly messing up their gig. I was a bit pissed so I went over to apologise. The guy said, it's ok and understood what happened. I think he was still buzzing from what he thought was a great gig. He even gave me the £20 which was good of him actually. I felt like I owed him one so I gave them a hand removing the gear from the stage. The only problem was, in my inebriated state, I was putting back the things they had just taken off! Another "Spanner" moment. Oh well, time to get out of there anyway in case they were cashing up. Cringeworthy but a good night and I actually made some money too.

It was my 21st birthday celebration on the nearest Saturday to my birthday in 1988. Kabuki Smiles were playing The Compasses as usual. It was always good natured, but there was usually a front row of hard looking skinheads, who were regulars and could be a bit of a handful. I wasn't watching the band as much as normal as it was my birthday. I was around the back when halfway through the set, Ade called someone to get me as I was needed. A plug kept coming out and he needed someone to hold it in or something. I was only too glad to help. I was up there, getting some stick not really knowing what was going on. The next thing I know, the old bill came in saying there was too much noise. This WPC came onto the stage and asked who was responsible for the racket. Everyone pointed at me. Oh shit – now I know what's going on.

This voluptuous non WPC, proceeded to take off her clothes. I mean, she was actually stunning but I hate these things. The 80s was full of Rolly Polly and Tarzan o grams. I thought they were tacky at the best of times. She asked me to take my shirt off. There were a dozen skinheads bellowing and another 90 people probably all shouting. I wasn't having it. I went up to the mic and said,

"You're all a bunch of wankers" and walked off.

Little did I know, they'd paid top dollar to get the best stripper, and she was supposed to go all the way, whatever that meant. Either way, I was outta there and Mr Unpopular for that evening.

There were some brilliant nights there though, and I'm still mates with a lot of people from those days. Ade used to get a fair bit of attention from the ladies, as he was ok looking and the frontman. I remember getting in the cab to go back to Peregrine Road. Ade was seeing someone at the time. There were 2 or 3 girls talking to us as we were waiting for the cab, flirting and stuff. We said, sorry, we've got to get back. As we got in the cab, in the mirror, the girls all opened up their coats to reveal fishnet stockings and suspenders. The driver nearly had a heart attack and couldn't believe it when we told him not to turn back!

We got to know a load of new people from the college, and got an invite to a New Year's Eve Party in Staines. Steve was a mate of the band's. I had driven to The Hart in case we went. I would've driven to the house party and left my car there (probably – it was the 80s) but Ade said we should hold out for something better. I wasn't so sure but as the evening went on, and a lot of people were elsewhere, he said we should probably go.

"Your car's in the carpark, isn't it?"

"Yes, but I ain't driving now."

He kept trying to get me to change my mind. I eventually said that if he wanted to drive it, he could but I'm not, I'd had way too much. As it was now a quarter to midnight, we decided to dash off down the London Road to Staines, him driving. The streets were empty. We got there just as the first bong of Big Ben chimed. It was great timing and everyone was really pleased to see us. Except Steve's dad who was a copper.

"Don't worry" Ade says,

"I've only had shandy and we'll pick it up in the morning!"

I don't think we even did that.

The only other thing that I can think of to do with Kabuki Smiles, was when I was working for this dry rot company. We were allowed to take the van home and use it locally. Well, the old van was out of use because a fire started in the cab area and it was burnt out. I think that was one of Ade's practical jokes, but it could easily have started from the pile of fag butts in the ashtray that I hadn't emptied. Either way, it was out of action and the hire company only had a tipper truck. A bit of a pain as you had to lift the heavy bags higher up but that was ok. I'd sometimes drive to the pub as I rarely had more than 3 or 4 pints on a week day. I wouldn't do that now or for the past 30 odd years but I can't deny that I did then.

I was leaving at chucking out time with Adrian. We noticed Dave and Ian from the band with a couple of their mates probably walking back from The King's Head. I pulled over and said do you want a lift? They jumped in the back, and I went round the roundabout to go back on myself, through the high street and past The Royal Hart where we'd just come from. Adrian meanwhile was pressing up on the "tipper" button. I was not wanting to draw attention to myself, as I may have been over the limit, so I was pressing it back down. Up and down, up and down. In the end I though bollocks and just left it up, flying around the corners with them, legs dangling behind in the rear-view mirror, shouting their heads off. It wasn't far and I pulled over to Dave and Ian's house. I was expecting them to go mad.

"Span, that was fucking brilliant!"

They wanted me to do it again. No way, I just want to get home as I'd already pushed my luck, as the old bill often cruised past at chucking out time. It was funny though.

There was one other incident. My parents were away. I thought it would be a good idea to invite everyone back after the pub. It wasn't that far away so once again I drove. I had an old Ford Escort. We came back with most of the band and girlfriends etc – all in my car. We counted everyone as they got out. 9 people in a Ford Escort. Is that a record? My older brother put a stop to the party when it was getting a bit lairy. Probably just as well.

There was another time when my van was out of action. I was told that the hire company only had a 7 and a half tonner. Not ideal, but you were allowed to drive them on your normal licence. I quite enjoyed driving around in it with the air brakes sounding like an 18-wheeler. I was king of the road. I had to drop off some bags of render to this house that some of the guys were working on. It was easy to load up as it had a hydraulic tail gate. The house wasn't accessible by road though. It was next to a small green. I was told that it would be ok to back on to the green as it wouldn't be for long as we unloaded. I got it into reverse and started driving blind, long before reversing cameras. Something was stopping me. I figured it was the kerb, so I gave it more revs and put my foot down to get up the kerb. It still wasn't happening. I tried a couple of more times when one of the workers ran out and yelled at me to stop. I got out to see what was happening. I had half knocked over a lamppost! It was at a 45-degree angle. Oops. We pushed it back up and stuck a few bricks in the hole that I'd made. Bingo – it stood up. I made my way back to the depot and got away with that one.

Playa De Las Americas

As I'm writing this, it has occurred to me that most of the incidents that I've recollected happened away from the pub. I guess it's the unusual experiences that stick in your mind. Also, every session pretty much down the Hart, had something that happened which could've probably gone in this book, but you were just living for the moment. It's about the people anyway, not the building.

Lisa's parents had a pretty nice time share apartment in Tenerife. We went there on our honeymoon, but also, the 2 of us went with another couple once before. I'll change their names as they had already pretty much split up at the time, but still wanted to go on holiday for the week. Let's call them Bill and Carol.

The holiday was good. Lots of swimming, going out in the evening to bars and restaurants. It was still a nice part of

Tenerife at the time. Just before the 18-30 mob descended upon it.

There was one incident that I have to tell though as it was so funny. We decided to take a trip out to the Water Park. It wasn't that far away and it had loads of pools and slides, including the highest water slide in Europe at that time apparently. We'd done a few of the smaller slides which were ok. I wasn't keen on when you fly down and get that winded feeling like when you drive over a steep bridge too fast, but it was all good fun. Of course, Bill wanted to go down the ridiculously big chute. It was so high, I wasn't keen.

Eventually, I agreed that I would do it if he did first. I'm not one to back down so he was ok with that. Up he went, higher and higher in his mustard speedos. Never a good look if you ask me. It got to the point where myself, Lisa and Carol were at the bottom chatting away waiting for him to come down. It was so high that there was no way of seeing him until he was half way down.

"Here he comes" says Carol.

Sure enough, he came whizzing down and along the level bit at the end which slows you down.

"That was brilliant!" he exclaims still visually buzzing from his experience. Then, there was a long pause and his smiles turned to apprehension as he stood up.

"Hang on a minute" he whispers.

"Eurgh, I think I've shit meself."

I couldn't see anything. Then he turned around, accompanied by trickles of brown water running down the back of his legs.

"Yes, I think you have!" I said laughing.

"NOOOOO!"

With that he looked around and jumped straight into the nearest pool. I think it was a kiddie's pool, so there was probably plenty of shit and piss in there already. We were still laughing. Well, the two girls were. Then I realised I still had to go and do it. Gulp. I climbed and climbed the deceptively and seemingly never-ending steps. It seemed even higher when you were at the top. The wind blowing a warm gale, but there was no going back now.

I'm glad to say, I managed it without incident, but half way down, there's a small jump. It bloody well hurt my back when landing, and yes, the water does go everywhere, but for once, I was not the butt of the joke, and made it back down safely, thankfully without shitting myself.

Steve And Debbie's

Fireworks Party

"If ever there were two words in the English dictionary that shouldn't go together, it's 'fireworks' and 'party' – Mike Slifkin, 27th February, 2021."

That's when I initially started to write this book. Over 3 years ago! Steve and Debbie were brilliant company down the Hart. They ran Martins, the newsagent's, dead opposite the pub. When they arrived from Southampton, they just fitted in perfectly. Normally people needed a little while to settle in, because there were lots of strong personalities down there. One minute they weren't there, then they were, and they loved socialising as we all did, but they were really good at it. Within days it seemed like they had been regulars for years.

I imagine that it was after a year or two of going down there, that they decided to have a fireworks party in their small garden around the back of the shop. We all clubbed in and they probably got the fireworks at cost price. I don't know but there were loads there. Being November 5th, you had to wait until it got dark. That's no problem, more drinking time. This is where things started to go wrong.

When the evening began, Steve was being very professional, lighting them and off they'd go one at a time. We'd all been drinking for a few hours now though, and it was a bit slow. Not for long however, as it wasn't long before we were all grabbing rockets, and just lighting them in our hands. Idiots I know but it was great feeling the reverse thrust as they shot off!

I saw Adrian do some, then I did a few. Before you knew it, it seemed like everyone was, except Debbie who was getting a bit pissed off with our obvious disregard to the fireworks code.

Not only this, but they had a couple of dogs in kennels at the other end of the garden. Again, not a brilliant idea. Still, the dogs didn't seem to mind. Well, that was until someone sent a stray rocket off which landed on the kennel roof, which in turn started a small fire. No harm was done – to the dogs at least, and I don't know who it was that did it. I'm sure it was accidental, but just for the record - it definitely wasn't me. Party prematurely ended and lessons learnt all round. Bloody hell, we could be stupid at times, but that was particularly stupid it has to be said.

Clive's Birthday Bash

This might surprise a few of you, but I actually went to a QPR match once. It was 23rd December 1995, and it was my first ever football match. As mentioned earlier, I was put off going to football matches by the violence. I was still supporting Liverpool in those days. Brentford were always my second team. The first time I saw Brentford, was losing the play off final at Wembley on 25th May 1997.

I feel that I should explain. My mum, dad and brother all grew up supporting Arsenal, with Brentford as their second team, as they were the nearest team to where we now lived. I was nuts on football like most boys in the 70s. As a kid, I didn't really get on with my older brother though, so there was no way that I was going to support a team that he supported. Football had changed from when my dad was younger, and he never liked the language on the terraces. He was quite old fashioned. I'm a couple of years younger than my brother and never got the opportunity to go, and to be honest, I wasn't that bothered. I just liked playing the game, bought Shoot magazine and Roy Of The Rovers. I also enjoyed watching the highlights on Match Of The Day Saturday and The Big Match on Sunday afternoon presented by Jimmy Hill and Brian Moore respectively. In the 70s and 80s all you ever heard about was violence at football matches, so that really did put me off. I was more into music by now anyway.

That is probably why I didn't mind going to Loftus Road. It was Clive's birthday and we were going to make a day of it. Clive lived quite close to me at the time, and we met at the corner shop on the way to the station. I'm not sure if The Hart was open but we met up with about 10 other mates or QPR fans on the way. Some others would meet us up in London in the evening after the game including Lisa.

Well, it was just one of those days I'll never forget, and for once I remember it quite clearly.

The first thing I remember, is when we got near the ground, we went into a big football pub on the White City Estate called The Springbok. The White City Estate was on South Africa Road so I guess that's the connection. It was full of Villa fans. I remember saying to Clive or Stav,

"Why are we in here?"

It was my first game and I was very wary of football hooligans.

"Just keep your head down – it's the nearest pub to the ground." I was told.

Villa fans were jumping on the tables, singing football songs, and glasses were getting smashed. I think there was a small scuffle at one point amongst themselves. It was known to be a pub for away supporters. It got a bit lairy in there so we left after a couple of pints.

The match itself was the funniest ever. I'm not just saying this, but QPR were getting mullered from the off. They were getting absolutely battered, but the ball would just not go in for Villa. Kevin Gallen got a breakaway goal and they hung on for a one nil win. Villa hit the woodwork countless times and Jurgen Sommer, the QPR goalie was man of the match in my opinion. Looking back, there were some famous names on the pitch. Gareth Southgate for one.

Clive, Craig, Stav, Neil and his girlfriend were there. I think Mickey and Lee were too and everyone was buzzing after the win, so it was off to The Moon On The Green to celebrate. I think this is where we met up with everyone else.

No-one really wanted to stay there all night. We'd all had a few by now. That said, it was Clive's birthday and it was far too early to head back to The Hart. A few people were wondering what to do. I remember suggesting that we should go into the West End to The Comedy Store, as I'd

been once before with Adrian and it was a good laugh.
Everyone pretty much seemed up for that so we headed
over to Leicester Square. This is where it gets a bit random.
There were only tickets for the late-night show. Not
everyone was up for that so I think one or two went home.
There was still a good 12 to 15 of us though. Whilst we
waited, we saw a bar nearby. It looked like a hotel bar but I
don't think it was. It was pretty posh for us, but we got in
and headed right down the end to get the drinks in.

We were all talking when I noticed this young lady playing
background music on the piano. She was really good. There
was a little tray on the piano for tips. After she finished, I
strolled up to her. She was really approachable and seemed
pleased that someone took notice of her.

"Do you do requests?" I asked.

I think she said something like it depends what it is or
something and she looked at the tips tray. I put a pound

coin in and said to her that I liked punk music, and the only thing that I can think of with piano is "I Don't Like Mondays" by The Boomtown Rats. She smiled and went straight into the Johnny Fingers intro – Dong Dong Dong Dong – DUH DUH DUH – brilliant! She played it perfectly throughout.

I went back to the bar but I'm not sure that the others even noticed at first. I went back to her after it had finished and said,

"That was excellent. Can you do Ever Fallen In Love?"

To this day, she probably gave the best answer I've ever had to a question.

"Fine Young Cannibals or Buzzcocks version?"

"Buzzcocks of course!" I replied and she started playing it. I gave her another pound and went back and told everyone.

"She can play anything. All you have to do is give her a pound each time."

I can't remember what else she played but everyone was requesting stuff, giving her a pound each time and she would play it. There was nothing she didn't know. She even said,

"You don't have to put a pound in every time you know."

We were more than happy to do so. For years we all thought it might have been Tori Amos, but doing some research for this book, I found out that it probably wasn't as she broke through a bit earlier. She looked like her though. Maybe she was doing a bit on the side to keep her hand in!

Comedy Store time. We were the first ones in. It's only small in there and I went straight to the front and sat down. Not everyone was quite so keen to be so close, but we'd all had a few so I thought what's the worst that could happen? I can't remember who was on that night, but Phil Jupitus did a turn and was the compare. He was quite well known but it wouldn't be for another 11 months before he was a team captain on Never Mind The Buzzcocks. I was a fan of his though and sometimes listened to his Greater London Radio show on a Saturday morning. We were pretty pissed by now and a few were heckling. Phil Jupitus gave back much more than he got. Neil, who was a bit of a twat at the best of times, kept retaliating by calling him a fat bastard or words to that effect. Neil came off much worse in this sparring match of words and whit. These comedians are used to the late weekend crowd.

In between sets, there's always a break to go to the loo or get a drink. Phil had come off stage and was talking to a young couple. We were all talking amongst ourselves when I decided to get up and wander over to him. I could see everyone wondering what I was up to. I thought I'd say hello so I waited by the pillar trying to catch his eye. He looked at me and said to the other two,

"Oh, I've got to go" and he came over to me for a chat.

He said something like,

"Thank fuck you came over. I was getting bored shitless with those two" and laughed.

He wasn't being mean. I think they were a bit Nigel and Doreen if you know what I mean. He said,

"You're with that lot over there in the front, aren't you?"

I said "Yes, it's been brilliant" which it was.

"I wasn't sure if I went too far. There's a lot of you!"

I reassured him that everyone was loving it, except Neil who we don't like anyway. I looked over and Neil was now asleep in his chair.

I could tell that everyone was looking over wondering what was going on. I told him that I sometimes listen to his radio show. It was really good. He'd play some new stuff mixed in with some punk and ska. Music that I liked. I told him that I loved an XTC cover he was playing at the time. He looked genuinely pleased that someone actually listened. I asked him where he got it from and he told me Tower Records or somewhere and then said,

"Actually, follow me."

Next thing you know, I'm off walking backstage with him, and he actually had a cd of it with him in his dressing room. We had a brief chat and he said,

"Shit, I better get back on" so we shook hands, I sat down and he did the next bit of comparing and that was that. All my mates were wondering what the fuck was going on! Oh, and Neil got both barrels for the second half.

It really was a great day out from when QPR were still a bigger team than Brentford. It was long time ago. Had to get that in.

From Cornwall To The Norfolk Broads

I'd been going out with Lisa for a good couple of years now. We'd already been on holiday to Tenerife as previously mentioned. We went to the Norfolk Broads, but the year before that, we went to Helston in Cornwall. That was a drama in itself. We stayed on a farm in a cute little cottage. It was absolutely freezing on the first day. The husband and wife owners, quickly showed us around and left us to it. The husband said he would pop by in the morning to bring us some fresh milk and to make sure that everything was alright.

It was tiny but really cosy. There was a small kitchen and a front room. Upstairs just had a bedroom and loo. Well, we were both wet behind the ears. All I knew, was that it was freezing, and the only heating was from a nice open fire. I'd always loved the idea of an open fire. Now I know I'm going to make myself look very silly, but I was trying to light these bloody logs with a match!

"It won't bloody light" I kept saying. I didn't realise that you needed firelighters and kindling to get it going. That was a bit embarrassing the next day when it was explained to me. You live and learn.

I think it was only a short break thankfully, because the next day, we thought we would hire a couple of bikes out from a little place around the corner that we'd seen. The idea being that we would have a nice cycle ride around the idyllic country lanes. When we hired the bikes, the owner gave us a trail to follow with a map. He gave us three options of difficulty. We both hadn't ridden a bike since we were young teens, so we sheepishly asked for the basic route. He said that it should take us about an hour if we go at a steady rate. That sounded good to us so off we went.

Now, Cornwall is very hilly in places. This bit of Cornwall had a special name. It was called "fucking ridiculously hilly!" It was so steep that even in first gear, you had to get off and walk the bike up the hill. It was actually a much warmer day and we were already knackered. I was still up for giving it a go but Lisa was completely fed up by now.

"There's a pub back there" she said. "Let's get a drink first." I think she meant a soft drink.

Well, back then especially, you didn't need to ask me twice. We parked up the bikes, spent the next 2 hours in the pub, and then dropped the bikes back off 5 minutes around the corner. "How was the ride?"

"Yes, not too bad" we lied trying to keep the smell of booze in. Well, we were on holiday.

Then we went for a walk and got lost in the fields. It must've taken us 3 hours to find our way back to the farm, so we did get our exercise in the end. Karma.

The holiday that I really wanted to talk about was our week-long boat trip around the Norfolk Broads. It didn't bode well. After the 123mile, 3 hour trip, we pulled in to the boatyard and got a puncture on their gravel driveway. I had roadside insurance so I should've just called up the AA or whoever I was then with, and got them to change the tyre there and then, but that would've be too easy. It was Benjamin Franklin who once said "Don't put off until tomorrow what you can do today."

It was me who said "I'll do it later."

We booked ourselves in. The owner asked us if we'd had any boating experience, and if he wanted him to show us the ropes.

"Er, yes." I said. "I've never driven a boat."

We got in. It was pretty small considering we were supposed to live on it for the next week. Below deck was a small bed, a tiny loo and kitchenette type arrangement. Above, were the controls and a little place to sit on the front behind a rail. It was on a budget and was fine for what we needed. We weren't sure what to expect, but he whizzed us around the harbour and pretty much left us to it.

Wet behind the ears is a phrase that keeps popping up from when I was still a teenager. I just wasn't worldly wise and had a lot to learn. Both of us really. I should state that whilst I enjoyed elements of this little holiday, there were too many things that ruined it. I think the easiest thing, is to do them in order as far as I can remember.

The first thing was, we didn't know how to change the toilet when it was full. The guy did mention something but it went in one ear, and out the other. This wouldn't be so bad if we hadn't found out that the previous users, hadn't cleaned it out before we hired it. It was already half full.

After day 3, the boat smelt of other people's stale poo! No problem, we just stuck loads of the blue stuff down there as the boat was only closed at night when we were asleep. I'm heaving now just at the thought. It now smelt like school toilets. Heavy bleach with an underlying smell of week old faeces.

No matter. Onwards and upwards. We had a decent map and we were going to head towards the town of Norwich for our first trip. There were only 2 locks to navigate. Should be a good way of learning how to get through them. It was great fun bobbing along, people waving as we were making our way. All of a sudden, I thought I felt the boat hitting the river bed. I checked with Lisa who was navigating, but she assured me that we should be there soon. I ploughed on. It was about 10 minutes later when the engine started letting off steam. I stopped, looked closely at the map and couldn't believe it. It was upside down. Now it was me that was letting off steam. We had our first argument. If it wasn't the fact that we were blowing up the engine and that we'd just wasted 3 hours going the wrong way, I may have found it funny. Time for a rest. For us and the poor little boat.

We turned the boat around, nearly ran aground again in the same place. Overheated, waited, carried on and eventually, found somewhere to moor up for the night not that far from where we started.

The next morning, we carried on going the right way, and began our holiday in earnest. The only good thing, was that the weather was perfect. Dry and sunny but not baking. We made the best of it and had a pretty good day. All I wanted to do was find a pub and moor up for lunch and a few beers. Every time we tried to park the boat, it was a nightmare. You're supposed to reverse in and do the back first, Lisa would jump out, tie us up and the front should naturally swing round on its own volition. I think this happened a few times during the week. It was a nightmare. We decided to find Norwich and just stay in that area avoiding the locks because they were a pain too. I've since learned that it's virtually lock free these days. I'd actually love to spend a few days there now I'm older, but every time I mention it, Lisa has other ideas. Too many bad memories. Here's another.

We'd had a long day and couldn't find any space to moor up. Eventually we found somewhere. It was a small spot behind this much bigger boat. There was only one stand so the guys in front, let us tie the other end to their boat. Excellent. They were a bunch of Welsh guys and a couple of girls. I knew this because they had tied up the Welsh flag on their boat. They seemed nice enough, so job done. We were sorted and took a walk in to Norwich. Everywhere was rammed and full of clubs and tacky bars. Not our thing at all so we went back to the boat and called it a night at about 10pm.

The next thing we know, there's loads of shouting and screaming. To be honest, it was really noisy all night. I think we were quite near a nightclub, so we were probably half awake anyway. I got up and peeked above deck. Shit, we were floating away from our mooring along with the Welsh boat. Some bastard must have seen the Welsh dragon on the flag, and decided that it would be hilarious to untie them. They untied us as well though, as we were attached to them and floating aimlessly around in the dark. About 3 of them had managed to get on board their boat but we had now become unattached to them. This big fella said,

"Don't worry, I've got a rope."

Now the thing with alcohol, it can sometimes make you think that you can do things that in reality you cannot. Jumping five feet onto our boat was one of them. Maybe he should've just thrown me the rope.

The next thing I know, he has attempted to leap onto our boat but missed it by about 2 feet. Then next thing we hear is the inevitable SPLASH!

He's in the drink. I must admit, I went from a tired panic to nervy laughter, as I wasn't sure how he was gonna react. All his mates started pissing themselves. To be fair, it was really good of him, and he still tied us up and swam back to the bank, where they all made sure both boats were well tied up. It was all a bit surreal. We couldn't thank him enough. His mates kept on giving him loads of stick and eventually we managed to get some shut eye.

It must've only been a few hours later, when Lisa woke up half on top of me. I thought my luck was in, but no, she was panicking thinking that the boat was sinking. It was not sinking; we were at about a 45-degree angle. I got up and sure enough, the Welsh blokes hadn't allowed for any slack seeing as it was tidal. We were about an hour away from dangling in mid air due to the rope being too short. For

220

fuck's sake. I somehow managed to scramble out, untie us, and we cleared off.

I didn't fancy having any awkward conversations with the occupants on the other boat. I was tired. Nowadays, I'd have definitely stayed and it would've been funny seeing them get up and talking about the previous evening's escapades.

We may have had a day where nothing eventful happened, but this would not last. It was a lovely sunny day and we found this picturesque marina, where you could moor up and walk into the village. Seemed like a good idea. Lisa was getting the hang of tying up the boat now, and I too got the hang of mooring up if that's the correct expression. Lisa would jump out of the back and tie it up, and I'd jump off at the end and do the front.

On this occasion, the current was really fast. I mean *really* fast. I managed to get the back in, Lisa jumped off, but the front wouldn't swing round. In a panic, she let go of the rope as the current was too strong. I was on my own. I threw her the rope but she didn't have the strength to hold it due to the current.

I'd already killed the engine. No problem, I'd just start her up again and have another go. The only problem was, it wouldn't fire up. This hadn't happened before. I'm floating away now quite fast in this current, and the bloody thing would not start. Again – nothing. Again – nothing. By now, I'm bashing into really expensive boats which were moored up all along this promenade. Lisa is shouting, crying – panicking. I'm shouting and panicking. It's a sunny, Saturday afternoon. The place is packed. BANG – I've hit another £200,000 boat. "Sorry!" "SHIT, SHIT, SHIT!" I've given up trying to start her up now. I'm going at a rate of knots towards this bridge. I'd be smashed to smithereens. I had about a minute before I was gonna bail out and let it smash.

I had images of those Disney films where you'd be floating on a log in a current, when suddenly there would be a massive waterfall. Still, this was The Norfolk Broads not The Niagara Falls. Stay calm.

Suddenly, Lisa's commotion, and the banging of the boat into other boats attracted some attention from onlookers. Luckily there was a Norfolk Broads volunteer nearby. You'd get them every now and again, normally near a lock or a mooring. He was running alongside me on the promenade bit.

"It won't start" I'm shouting.

"Throw me the rope" he shouted back.

The bridge is getting larger and larger. I manage to quickly haul in the now wet rope and with all my might, I chucked it over. He leant forward to grab it, but it just wasn't close enough. I'm proper panicking now and look like giving up. "Try again!" he yelled. I reeled in the rope for one last try. I scooped it up, threw it over, and with the excess adrenalin pumping through my veins, I managed to give it a bit more oomph and he somehow just managed to get hold of it. Thank fuck for that. With some help from people nearby, they managed to pull me in, just before I hit the bridge. This was not fun. However, I couldn't thank him enough.

He was just about to jump on board when, just in time, I realised something. There was a reason why the boat wouldn't start. I'd flicked on the safety switch. I always did this when we moored somewhere, for safety reasons. In the panic, I'd forgotten to switch it back off to enable the engine to start. I discreetly flicked the switch as he jumped on board and of course, it started up straight away when he pressed the button.

"That's funny" I said. "Oh well – at least it works now." The worst thing was doing the walk of shame along the promenade, again apologising for all the boats I'd hit.

Actually, everyone was very good about it. I felt terrible.

Gigs (Part 2)

By now, I was a fairly regular gig goer. I'd seen loads of bands at The Compasses, Numan and The Stranglers every year at Hammersmith or Guildford. Sometimes both, plus the occasional other gig. I got to see The Cure in December 1987, Depeche Mode too both at Wembley. A highlight was Depeche Mode, co headlining with The Sisters Of Mercy at Crystal Palace in 1993. I never really kept ticket stubs but I wish that I did now. Other bands that I can remember seeing in the late 80s, were The Creatures, The Cocteau Twins, Jesus Jones and I was roped into seeing All About Eve. I nearly fell asleep. Dullest band I've ever seen live.

By the 90s it was still mainly Gary Numan and The Stranglers, although I did go to the first Madstock with Lisa on the second day, August 9th 1992. I had my Smiths t-shirt on as Morrissey was supporting, and although I loved Madness, I was more of a Morrissey fan. As soon as we got in, there was a crowd of Mozza fanatics. One came over to me crying her eyes out.

"He's not playing today as he got coined off last night."

As it turned out, most support bands also got the same treatment. I was a bit pissed off but I wasn't going to let that ruin my first festival type experience. We had a mooch about, got a bite to eat and had a couple of beers, then we went over to see the various support bands.

Gallon Drunk and Flowered Up were OK, and Ian Dury was always entertaining. Madness were brilliant playing most of their classic singles.

As we were leaving, we accidentally found our way into the backstage area. I saw John Lydon and said to Lisa, "Let's try and get a free beer and find out who we can see."

It had been a long day though and she wanted to get back home so we didn't stay long. A shame.

What I'm really leading up to though, is what I would say was my moment of madness – quite literally.

It was to be 6th August 1994, when most of the younger members of The Royal Hart, decided that we should hire a full sized 40-seater coach and go to Madstock. As previously mentioned, myself and Lisa had already been before. Some of the others may also have been, but this year it was going to be immense.

We would all meet the night before in the Hart to get into the mood. I left early for some reason. It was agreed about a week previously that we would all dress up and look the part.

I found out the next day that someone had brought some clippers with them on the Friday before, and everyone was taking it in turns to sit in the chair in the corner and get a number one haircut. I'm glad I left early.

It was a warm Saturday afternoon. We were in the pub or mingling outside waiting for the coach to turn up. I guess I'd already had 3 or 4 pints when my mother-in-law walked past. There was me with pork pie hat on, grandad shirt and red braces, already 2 and a half sheets to the wind, hanging out with about 15 others who all looked similar. She seemed a bit intimidated and after some small talk, she carried on with her shopping. I don't blame her.

Eventually, the coach turned up and we all piled in. As usual, some were just finishing a pint, whilst others had just started. This would go on for a while as drinking speed is difficult to synchronise. Someone made the decision to say we're leaving. Drink up or stay behind.

As you can imagine, everyone was up for it and on good form. All taking the piss out of each other and generally having a laugh. Off we went on a jolly boys outing.

The driver was clueless though and kept taking us the wrong way. I'd had enough – I was busting for a piss. We had already stopped once earlier but I was ok then as we were nearly there. Like I say, the driver went all around the houses and I needed to go now – badly.

I got him to stop outside a pub.

"Hurry up or we'll leave you here."

I ran into the pub, past the bar, to the gents. Luxury. It went on and on and on. I remember thinking that they probably will bugger off because I hate to be so graphic, but it was one of those pisses that just didn't seem to stop. I genuinely thought they'd probably left me there when I got out but I didn't care. Heaven.

No, there it was like a beacon. I felt great now. I got back on board and everyone was either shouting or cheering that I had finally finished. This sounds weird but it was a great reaction and I think that started me off on one of my most bonkers days ever. I just didn't care that day. Getting all the attention definitely triggered something inside me.

We eventually got there. It seemed different to last time. Like I say, we were all well up for it. We went to the beer tent right at the back. You had this weird ticketing system, where you had to queue to buy a ticket, and then queue once again to get a beer with your ticket. A stupid idea, so most of us would get 2 pints each at a time to save queueing. We'd all had a fair few already plus topping up from the night before, so it didn't take long before we were all well oiled. There's also something about wearing different clothes to what you would normally wear. I guess like fancy dress, and there was something in the air that day. There was a good vibe. Before you knew it, about 10 of us were having shoulder carry fights right at the back, probably while Aswad were on. Good background music for shoulder carry fights! It was such a laugh. It bloody hurt when you fell off someone's shoulders though. Unless you were on Syd's because he's only a short arse!

This went on for half an hour or so until we were all knackered and had enough. I'm not sure how this next bit started. I think I was just pissing about throwing a bit of my pint into the air and trying to catch it. I got egged on and did it until I ran out of beer. Before you knew it, someone else threw theirs in the air, I would try and drink it before it landed on the grass.

After a little while, more and more people were doing this. I was in the middle of about 20 or so people, some strangers who had queued up twice, just so that they could pay over the odds to chuck their beer at some twat they'd never met before. It created quite a scene.

"My go." Someone would shout and then everyone would go,

"Woooooooaaaaaaaahhhhhhhh" and throw the beer in the air whilst holding on to the plastic pint container, and I'd try and drink it. Although I was only getting a fraction of the beer each time, I was getting pretty shitfaced - and very wet. The bit that everyone says really made them laugh, was when this girl did it. I was now in the middle of about 30 people. She threw it in the air, I caught some of it in my mouth, spat it out and yelled,

"Eugh, who threw the cider?" I didn't like cider back then.

Everyone laughed and pointed at this poor girl.

"Sorry, it was me" she meekly said.

I'd noticed that Ian Dury had started. I really wanted to see him again, so myself, Lisa and a few others made our way to the front. I was buzzing now, having had all the attention for the past half an hour plus copious amounts of booze.

The only problem was, it was now rammed. When we got as far as we could get, I shouted out,

"Let me through, I want to see my brother."

I must've been convincing.

"Let him through, he's Ian Dury's brother!"

We actually got within the first three rows, excellent. The Blockheads always started with Wake Up And Make Love With Me which is quite a slow number from the New Boots And Panties album, so that helped. Then, it was Billericay Dickie which isn't a fast track but everyone loves it. The place went mad. A bit like The Pistols gig in Crystal Palace which I'll get to later. We found ourselves moving involuntarily with the crowd. It wasn't scary though, just a bit unnerving. What I didn't like, yet still found fascinating, was when we were moving without our feet touching the ground. It was like swimming standing up - very strange. We lasted a little while and then I thought better of it

having Lisa up there with me, so we made our way back
through everyone we got past earlier. Ian Dury always did a
thing where he went "Oi Oi" and the crowd would respond
back with the same. I just went past everyone, taking my
hat off and going "Oi Oi." It seemed to go down well and I
got lots of responses. We got back to the others reasonably
unscathed.

Ian Dury And The Blockheads were brilliant as always. By
now, a load of pretty mean looking original skinheads had
made their way to the back and side, and had scrambled up
onto the tent roofing swaying about in time to the music.
Meanwhile, I saw this really tall, thuggish looking skin on
his own smoking a fag. I was still buzzing and liked a
challenge, so I moseyed up to him like John Wayne
skulking into a saloon bar. I took off my hat and went "Oi
Oi." I don't know why really.

I was just having a mad day plus the alcohol. He totally
blanked me. I could tell that there were about 10 or 15 of

The Royal Hart lot looking on in the background. OK I thought. I better have another go "Oi Oi" a little louder and a little closer this time. Some might say more intimidatingly, but not from me. He wasn't having any of it. He stood his ground firmly looking at me like the shit from under his 14 hole oxblood Dr Martens boots. Well, I was standing my ground too. There was no way back now, even if it meant I'd get my teeth smashed in. I went right up to his face, took my pork pie hat off and went "OI, OI!"

I was ready for the worst. I mean, if he hit me, it wouldn't have hurt until the morning anyway. Then he swallowed, shrugged and sheepishly replied in his deep baritone voice,

"Oi oi" and that was that.

I walked back to my mates victorious, like Wellington after The Battle Of Waterloo. I later found out that they were also expecting me to get battered, and were getting ready just in case. Maybe the skinhead saw them and thought better of it. Who knows? It was very silly but also very funny at the time. By now, it was time for Madness.

They were excellent as always. I've seen them a fair few times over the years and they always put on a good show. They've got a great back catalogue of singles, and Suggs is just a really good frontman, always coming out with some witty one liners. After the first track I remember him saying "Have we got time for just one more?" Very amusing. I think this was the gig where everyone was jumping up and down in unison, to the ska beat and it caused a 4.1 earthquake on the Richter scale. I reckon if we all went know, it would be more like an 8.

The best outdoor gig I've ever been to though, was probably The Sex Pistols comeback at Finsbury Park on June 23rd 1996. I went with a mate from The Royal Hart. Ray, the one who didn't have his face in the omelette at The Kismet. Ray was more into rock music and is a good

20 years older than me. That didn't stop him seeing AC/DC at Wembley on the Friday, Madstock all dayer on the Saturday (different to the previously mentioned Madstock event), and here we were, back again for a full day at Finsbury Park to see the reformed Sex Pistols.

The funny thing about Madness on the previous day (Saturday) was that we were in the pub watching England versus Spain in the Euro 96 Quarter-Finals. This was before we entered into the festival area, somewhere in Finsbury Park near the venue. It wasn't the best match. It finished 0-0 but we won 4-2 on penalties for once. The place went mental. They probably heard us in Wembley only a few miles away. Then, loads of rude girls and nutty boys left the pub very pissed and very happy. The one thing I remember, is walking on to the zebra crossing. In front of us were about 5 blokes doing the nutty boys march on the zebra crossing. It was so funny. They got about half way across, doing it perfectly, and then would do it backwards.

Cars were hooting, and they must've done this for what seemed like five minutes, going back and forth, generating loads of onlookers laughing, until cars got impatient and just drove through. It was a brilliant start to an eventful weekend.

The Pistols did play a festival and another gig on the previous 2 days in Europe, but this was pretty much the first gig they'd done since January 14th 1978. The infamous "Ever get the feeling you've been cheated" gig declared by Johnny at Winterland in San Francisco.

I think myself and Ray went straight there as we would've had a lot to drink at Madstock on the previous day. It seemed weird going back to Finsbury Park the day after. I bet we weren't the only ones though.

I'm pretty sure that we missed a few of the support bands which is a shame, but we knew it was going to be a long day. We missed Skunk Anansie, 60ft Dolls, 3 Colours Red who would've had Chris McCormack on guitar who later would be a guitarist for Gary Numan for a few years.

We came in just as The Wildhearts were finishing. I don't remember seeing Stiff Little Fingers which is weird, as I would've loved to have seen them. We were pretty chilled near the back having a few beers chatting and listening to Buzzcocks who were great. I then suggested that we should head up to the front to see Iggy Pop, and stay up there for the Pistols, who were on straight after, so we did. It was bit mental up there. Bottles of piss were being launched and we dodged a few, more out of luck than judgement. I like Iggy but I'm not a massive fan. I had seen him once before with Ray and he was a nutter live so I was looking forward to it. I wasn't disappointed. He was nearly 50 and was still throwing himself around the stage. At one point he dived off going over mine and Ray's head into a bunch of fans behind us. At this point it went completely mad and I lost contact with Ray.

I decided to stay there and wait until The Sex Pistols came on. All the hype was that it was going to be a bit of a pantomime and ruin their legacy, and that they were just going to take the money and run. I thought they always were a bit of a pantomime, so wasn't bothered about that, but I did want them to put on a good event.

The next thing we knew, Gareth Southgate and Stuart Pearce turned up on stage to an amazing ovation, fresh from beating Spain yesterday. Pearce had managed to persuade Terry Venables to let him out, if he took Gareth with him as a chaperone. I don't think Gareth had ever been to a gig before, and certainly not a punk one. It was well known that Psycho loved punk and I'd seen him at Stranglers gigs before. Here they were on stage, announcing The Sex Pistols with a giant backdrop of the Daily Mail headline "The Filth And The Fury" and "Filthy Lucre."

I couldn't believe it when The Pistols came on, looking great and going straight into Bodies, their most outrageous song, and one of my favourites. The sound was incredible. So much for the critics. They were not trying to make a quick buck. They'd spent a lot of money on this PA. It was immense and knocked you off your feet. Johnny was great up front.

"Fat, Forty And Back!" he spat out. It was just a brilliant gig. It was being filmed. At one point he pushed a cameraman and he was inches from falling off the stage backwards. It was exciting. All of Never Mind The Bollocks plus b sides were played, finishing on the second encore with No Fun.

I saw them another 3 times after this. They were always brilliant and put on a show. Once at Brixton Academy which was equally good, once at Crystal Palace which was a bit scary. It's the only time that I've been genuinely scared at a gig. It started well enough, And You Will Know

Us By The Trail Of The Dead were supporting. They were

inciting the crowd by being overly provocative. They got

coined off and I saw Johnny lurking to the side. I have a

very loud voice as certain people will testify. I shouted as

loud as I could,

 "JOHNNY!"

After doing this a couple of times he actually heard and

came over gesturing to me. He mouthed,

"What?"

Well, I didn't really have anything to say. I was just excited

so I gave him a thumbs up and he did the same. It was good

though and were all anticipating a great gig.

They came on and went straight into a cover of

Hawkwind's Silver Machine. It shouldn't have worked but

it just did. The place went absolutely mental. We were

pushed from side to side, back and forth. People getting

knocked over, accidentally stamped on. I'm all for punk

rock and anarchy but not when it hurts! I wasn't keen on this. After a few songs it wasn't getting any better. You couldn't enjoy it as all your attention and concentration was to stay on your feet. I thought bollocks to this and tried to get out. The problem was, it was like a vortex. I was the last droplet of water going down the plughole into the void. The void is the place where you get stamped on and crushed to death. I tried a couple of times to get out of the vortex. The music stopped. I used all of my strength to push my way out. Once you got past the outer casing of people, you were sent flying back out of the vortex to relative safety. Phew, I'm not doing that again. I spent the next 10 or 20 minutes finding mates who had done the same thing, and gathered my breath. I think there were some casualties that day and I'm not surprised.

The other time I saw The Sex Pistols was at Hammersmith Odeon, as I will always call it. It was packed and a decent gig, but not as good as the others. I was with some people who hadn't seen them before and they all loved it. It was my fourth time so maybe I was getting a bit blasé with it all. Still good though. We watched it from the back. All the seats downstairs had been removed so it was a purely standing gig. There were not enough toilets for the amount of people there. I started queueing for the loos but it was ridiculous. I decided to go in the stone stairwell in the fire exit. It was either that or piss myself. I noticed that I wasn't the only one to have this idea. There were about a dozen of us pissing away!

Luckily the place got revamped soon after for the Kate Bush gigs. There was no way Kate was going to put up with the smell of urine whilst she was running up that hill. I heard that she paid for it out of her profits. Fair play Kate.

Anyway, back to Finsbury Park. Once the gig was over, I made my way back to the nearest tube station. As you can imagine, it was mobbed in there. I was just about to go down the escalator when I got a tap on my shoulder. I turned around and there was Ray battering me with a rolled up poster he'd bought. We both laughed as the chances of bumping in to each other again was slim, but it meant we both had some company for the trip back home.

We negotiated the tube and got on the overground train back to Ashford. Ray had just done 3 big gigs on the trot. AC/DC, Madness and now The Sex Pistols and he was knackered. The thing with Ray, is that he's the biggest wind up merchant you'll ever meet. I noticed our conversation on the train was now waning, when he found a paper and started to read it. I could tell that he was just trying to hide his face whilst he took a nap. Now I know what he would've done if the cards were reversed, so every now and again, I'd pick up his rolled up poster, and prod him in the face like a kid would prod a half dead frog or something with a stick. He'd wake up for a second and then go back to sleep. Of course, I would continue to do this on and off as it was a very boring train journey home. Every now and again, he'd tense up like he was going to whack

me one and I would laugh. It's good to be annoying

sometimes. It rounded off an excellent weekend.

Bulgaria And More

Myself and Lisa had become good friends with Iain, or gay Iain as he was known, who was always knocking about with Jackie. He's the guy who had New York, Paris, London, Stanwell painted on to his van at the funeral.

Along with another couple down the pub, Jock and Lynne, we decided to go to Bulgaria. We were to meet up with another couple who were there already, Bernie and Helen. We had never met them before but had heard everything about them from Iain, and I was sure that we would all get on well. I think Iain organised it. We stayed in this really cheap place, but it was quite near to Bernie and Helen's much nicer hotel. I don't know what Bulgaria conjures up in your mind now, but 25 to 30 years ago, I wondered what

we were letting ourselves in for. I thought of it as a
Communist Eastern Bloc country that was full of snow.

It had opened up since 1990 though like a lot of other
places in eastern Europe. I was up for a change of scenery
as we all were, and it was cheap. Very cheap.

We all got to the airport and as per usual, once we got rid
of our luggage, we hit the bar. We didn't go mad but we
had a few. I wasn't that keen on flying back then, so a few
beers to settle the nerves always helped. We relaxed a bit
too much though and nearly missed our flight. It was like
we were in the Hart and we weren't concentrating.

The next thing I remember is that we were taxiing on the
runway on the rickety old Aeroflot aeroplane. When the
pilot put his foot down (this is a well-known aviation
expression) all the seats flew back from the acceleration.
There was nervous laughter all round, and once we were
airborne, we needed some more light refreshment to steady

the nerves, which had definitely come back by now. I was sat with Iain and Lisa. It was when myself and Iain had a tomato ketchup fight, that we realised that we were probably relaxed enough now.

We got there, and checked in our things to this grotty place. To be honest, I can't remember it at all, but others have reminded me how bad it was. A tiny pull-out bed etc etc.

I should say that my memory of Bulgaria is shaky at best, so my recollections may come across like a bad edit in a film. That's a film not movie. I hate the word movie. I do remember this tiny wooden bar. The service was rude at best. We were always polite but I guess they just weren't used to tourism back then. I like to think that things must've improved greatly in the last 30 years or so. The first thing we noticed was that local beer was about 20p a pint. It was drinkable, but we had our eye on this fizzy red wine called Black Sea Gold. The first few times we had it, we quite enjoyed it. Maybe it was the novelty of fizzy red wine, but that only lasted for the first few days. Iain got properly drunk on it one evening and he said that he lost sight in one eye. He was prone to exaggeration but it wouldn't have surprised me. It was rough.

We were there for a fortnight which was probably a week too long. For some reason, on the first night, a few of us got a cab to go somewhere. We managed to persuade the driver to take us. You were only supposed to carry 4 passengers, but there were 5 in our group. He said, if there are any police about, one of you must get down. Well, it was just our luck that he got pulled over. He was telling us not to worry as it's his fault. The intimidating police officer ordered us to get out. Guns are standard equipment out there so they didn't need to ask twice. Helen had gone into panic mode though and tried to hide in the foot well. The driver had asked us all to get out. The police were obviously going to give the car a once over, so I asked

Helen to get out as it looks worse trying to hide. She didn't respond so I said something like,

"Get out of the fucking car."

She did and the taxi driver got a fine and that was that. I don't know why they were so strict on it. Anyway, we gave him a good tip and he seemed ok with it all. Helen never let me live

it down though. For years after she would bring it up.

"The first time you ever saw me, you swore at me" etc etc. I did, and Helen, I'd do it again!

The one good thing about the place, was that in the Summer, it wasn't snowy at all. In fact, it was beautiful sunshine every day, and we stayed in an area called Golden Sands which lived up to its name. It really was lovely.

Myself and Lisa had recently become vegetarian, which we still are to this day. It was a nightmare trying to find something to eat. We lived off of a thing called shopska salad and chips mostly. Shopska salad was the first time we'd encountered feta cheese. It's everywhere now, isn't it?

This probably didn't help when drinking day and night but we managed somehow. The first full day on the beach was weird. We went for a walk and there were showers every now and again. You'd see people taking everything off to have a shower in the nude. It wasn't a nudist beach; it just didn't seem to bother them.

The funny thing though was when Jock decided to go parasailing. I refused to do it because I didn't like heights. I'm actually ok these days. There he was shouting to me in his broad Glaswegian accent, from about 400 feet in the air. I think Iain fancied a bit of this so he paid his money, got kitted out and was awaiting the boat to take him up. Now

Iain, back then was quite a large fella. In fact, Helen always called him "Bigness." The next thing, on a packed beach, the owner starts running along the sand when he saw Iain harnessed up.

"STOP, STOP. TOO MANY KILOS. TOO MANY KILOS!!!!!!"

Iain was mortified, but it was so funny seeing him have to unravel himself from the harness with everyone watching. The number of times we'd shout 'too many kilos' to him it's amazing that he never became anorexic. He did however have to stop. No parasailing for fat bastards. He is actually a lot slimmer these days.

We went over to Bernie and Helen's hotel one day. It started off nice and we had some lunch, shopska salad and chips, and hung around by the pool drinking beer. The weather however was a taking a turn for the worse, so we decided to go in to the hotel due to the thunderstorm brewing. We found a mini, indoor bowling alley in the basement of the hotel. That passed a bit of time but we soon got bored.

The next thing I remember is running through the hotel in just my pants. For the life of me I can't remember why, as it's so unlike me. Probably too much Black Sea Gold.

One thing I do remember about Bulgarian culture, is that you had to remember that nodding your head meant "no" and shaking your head meant "yes". I mean, that could confuse a stupid person. The girls came back terrified once. They went to an underground public toilet. When they walked up into the high street, they were greeted by a man with a rabbit. They made a fuss of the little bunny, however, he then got out a knife and wanted money or the little fluffy bunnykins would get it. Charming.

The nightlife was terrible. There were plenty of bars but you couldn't just go up to the bar and order. They would make you sit, watch some third-rate cabaret act, and then, eventually come round with someone to take your order. Then, they'd bugger off and eventually return with the drinks. Without any exaggeration, this could sometimes take half an hour or so because there were 8 of us.

We found a karaoke bar one day called Bonkers. It was anything but. However, we did our best to make it that way. It was a lot easier to get a beer in there and after a few, some of us would get some Dutch courage and have a go at singing. I can remember getting up and having a bash at Whip It by Devo. Very surreal, especially as my gout had kicked in and I could hardly walk. Shopshka salad followed by beer day and night would do that!

I don't know what it is with karaoke. I'm no singer, but when there's a karaoke bar, I get this uncontrollable urge (good pun Devo fans) to sing something ridiculous. On our honeymoon, we were walking along in the daytime, with Iain and Jackie who had joined us for the second week in

Tenerife. We sat down and had a beer. It happened to be a karaoke bar, and I chose Bohemian Rhapsody and the Sid Vicious version of My Way to sing!

Anyway, back to Bonkers in Bulgaria, Bernie's choice was Leader Of The Gang by you know who. Now, one thing with Bernie is that he doesn't do anything half heartedly. He *was* Gary Glitter up on that stage. He was doing all the moves and getting everyone involved. It really was good.

It was funny though. The next morning, we met Bernie and Helen for breakfast in their hotel. We had shopska salad – no chips. It's breakfast, I'm not an animal. Bernie was nursing a bad hangover when these kids came over shouting,

"Gary Glitter – do your Gary Glitter."

Of course, that has different connotations these days, but the last thing Bernie wanted to do was Gary Glitter, but he had a brief go. You gotta keep your public entertained at all times!

On our travels we found a curry house, and it was proposed that we should go there for the last evening.

We sat down. It was quite big in there. The food resembled curry and it was passable. As usual, there would be a cabaret. This time a daredevil magician. He had a bed of nails and asked for a volunteer to stand on him, whilst he lay on this bed. I'm sure you've all seen it countless times. Straight away, Iain who was probably over 20 stone back then, got up, half jokingly I think. This magician was game though, he beckoned him over and sure enough, he laid himself slowly over the nails, bare chested. Then Iain stepped on him. When most people do this, they gingerly step on trying to be as light as possible. Not Iain, he got on like he was climbing up the back of a Routemaster bus.

"Oof" "Aggh!" "Oof, oof!"

He did it, for about 3 seconds and was then told to get off. The brave (or foolish) magician got up, blood streaming down his back. His finale should've been downing a pint of water, in order for us to watch it spurt out from his nail holes, like in the cartoons. It put me right off my whateveritwas and rice.

Iain did love his food and cider back then. He once told me that after he'd had a bucket (his terminology for loads of ciders) he went next door to Tasty Bake for sausage and chips. Then, he walked down to the Kismet, sat in and had a full curry. After that, on the way home, he popped into the Chinese for a takeaway which he couldn't manage – til morning!

Having gotten to know Bernie and Helen in Bulgaria, we started to go to London with them every now and then. They already used to go 3 or 4 times a year with Iain. The three of them would sometimes go up to Covent Garden in the West End, have a few drinks and a Chinese in Chinatown before getting back late at night.

Iain must have asked us if we wanted to go one time, so we thought we'd try something different. Sometimes there would be Jackie, another Jackie and Pixie, maybe Dippy Helen and we'd make a day of it. Myself, Lisa and Iain would meet in the Royal Hart, maybe have a couple, and walk over the road to the train station. We would then meet Bernie and Helen in The Marquis Of Anglesey in Covent Garden more often than not.

We did this a few times. It always ended up very messy. Normally in Harry's Chinese restaurant. Of course, I did the Lazy Suzan thing one time, spinning the table around like a motorcycle doing the wheel of death, cutlery, bowls and god knows what spinning everywhere out of control from the centrifugal force. It had to be done and it was just the once, as tempting as it was to do it every time.

I remember once, we were hammered as per usual, but as was the case on Sundays, the pubs shut between 3 and 7pm. You had to get a bit resourceful sometimes in order to carry on drinking. Helen had found a way. There was a restaurant by a piazza somewhere, where you could sit outside, order the least amount of food possible, in order to get wine to go with it. Tortilla chips and dips were a favourite. So, we'd sit out there with a plate of tortillas between us and about 4 bottles of Cab Sav red wine. Ingenious.

Well, I was pretty bad at handling my drink back then. I wouldn't get violent or anything, but I could get cheeky and a bit provocative. Some might say being a bit of a dick. I think that's what I would say now looking back. The piazza was also where Capital Radio transmitted from. I had a real bee in my bonnet about Capital Radio at the time, and saw a security guard outside. Of course, he was just doing his job and I was being a twat. I asked him if he liked Capital Radio and he didn't answer. I gave him my verdict on said radio station. He then told me that he didn't really like it either. I remember telling him that he was prostituting himself by working for them. What a knob I could be. Too much wine and far too pompous. Mind you, it was a shit radio station and probably still is.

The other thing I squirm at looking back, was when we were on a zebra crossing, and an old Chinese lady was walking the other way. For reasons I will never know, I pinched her hat off her head! It was just there asking me to do it. The others saw me and were laughing when she quite rightly, turned round and gave me loads of Chinese verbals. I gave it back of course. The hat, not the verbals. Sorry security man and Chinese lady. We just used to get far too drunk.

There was one time when we were at Harry's in the middle of Chinatown awaiting our lovely food. Normally at the end of the evening, Bernie and Helen would be rowing. That's having a row, not coming back via the river

Thames! It would often nearly ruin a really good day out, and they did eventually go their separate ways after many years. The number of times we said we wouldn't go again because of it, but always did. I guess the good outweighed the bad. On this particular occasion though, Lisa decided to sit in between them from the off, in order to suffocate any possible arguing. This idea was good in principle, but in reality, she just got shouted at from all angles as if she wasn't there. It was so funny. I don't know why she didn't move but I'm glad she didn't. It just made it even funnier.

If I couldn't take my drink back then, Helen was much worse. There was a time when we were on the train home and she kicked off her probably expensive shoes. I'm not an expert on lady's shoes, but Helen liked the nice things in life, so I'm guessing they weren't cheap. This enabled me to pick one up whilst she wasn't looking. I'm not sure why, but she was going on about something so I warned her first.

"If you don't stop, I'm throwing it out of the window." I told her.

She didn't stop, so I threw it out of the window. Actually, I didn't but I pretended too. She started crying uncontrollably! Even when I got her shoe back and showed it to her, the damage was done and she carried on crying most of the way home anyway!

Another time, we left it a bit late, and the closest train out of Waterloo to Ashford, was to Sunbury, which is still a few miles away from home. She drunkenly said she'd order a cab from the phone box. Remember them? The rest of us were talking amongst ourselves for about 5 minutes, when Bernie thought he'd see how she was getting on. He opened the door, and there she was – half asleep. We always got home eventually somehow. We would have the best times but it always ended in tears.

As an aside and to bring it back into the realms of Gary Numan, which I like to do with most things, Iain and Bernie were both in the same class as Gary Numan at school in Ashford.

I asked Bernie if he had any memories so that I could put them in the book. It was a long time ago but he did say this,

"To be honest, I don't really remember him being disruptive or that badly behaved at school. As I recall, he was fairly quiet, kept himself to himself, but really into his music. Definitely not a sporty type, and I can't remember him being part of an obvious friendship group. I may be wrong on that assumption, as apart from sharing a classroom, our paths didn't really cross."

In the past, I remember Iain telling me that Gary Numan or Webb back then, got a lot of stick for wearing stack heeled boots that he'd he'd sprayed silver.

They were as surprised as anyone when he suddenly

appeared on Top Of The Pops.

Engerland Games

Whether it was the Euros or the World Cup, even qualifiers, there was no better place to watch England play football, than in the Royal Hart in the mid 90s. We used to watch games in the public half, but the pub got made into an open plan space at some point, which was a stupid idea, because it lost its atmosphere. It was however, great for football matches, because you could get more people in. Depending on the time of the match, we would normally get down there an hour or 2 early to get in the mood.

I guess I should start at Euro 96, which I'm sure you'll remember, was held in England. There was probably a good hundred of us squashed in to the pub for England's second group game against Scotland, including one Scottish bloke, Jock. He loved to give us all stick and the possibility of beating us in our own back yard, was just too much of an opportunity for him to miss. The place went mental when Shearer put us in to the lead. To be honest, I wasn't bothered about Jock being there either way. He was always a wind up, but a good bloke. I just wanted England to win as I always do, no matter who the opposition is. All was going well in the second half, until Tony Adams committed a foul in the area. Penalty to Scotland. The next bit, I don't remember but apparently, Jock was busy jumping up and down, giving it large, before the penalty was even taken. As we now know, McAllister missed the pen, or rather Seaman brilliantly saved it. He then booted it up field, and Gazza did the famous left foot, right foot, bang. Goal, 2-0, dentist chair etc etc. Apparently, Jock was still celebrating the Scotland penalty when he got covered in beer. I wish I saw that; I was glued to the screen.

It was probably when we next faced Scotland, after we won in the qualifiers, that this next anecdote begins. Over to Houndy.

"We were all in the pub watching Scotland v England, and we had put the England flag up in the pub after the game having won. I said to Ray,

'Shall we put that flag on Jock's roof?'

He obviously thought that this was a good idea, so we got my ladder, put it on the roof of Dean's car, who is Ray's son, and I went over to Steve (Jock) and Lynne's flat. Once we got there, I managed to get on to the roof, half pissed, and put the flag up. Steve and Lyne were in Scotland at the time. We left it there until he got back!"

I didn't know any of this until Houndy got in touch recently. Brilliant. Jock never went down the pub after that for England games!

It would've been amazing if we ever won anything at that time. The place would've gone berserk. I remember when Michael Owen announced himself to the world, when he scored that amazing, individual goal against Argentina. It was a great win and meant a lot after the hand of God incident, years previous. Myself and Craig were buzzing. We decided to get out of the pub, get a train to Richmond, and celebrate big time. It was only when we were walking up the high street singing,

"WE BEAT THE ONION BHAJIS, WE BEAT THE ONION BHAJIS!" when we noticed that no-one really cared, other than the odd smile. It then dawned on us, that Richmond is a bit posh, but also Rugby Union territory, as it sits right next to Twickenham Stadium. Not the afternoon we had in mind, but I'm sure we still enjoyed ourselves.

There was another time, after an England win, when it was a hot, summer's day, so a few of us went outside after the match. Cars were tooting as they went by. Then, these 2 rather nice girls pulled over, lifted up their tops and gave us an eyeful of their tits. Classy.

Of course, it was always a terrible day out when we inevitably lost, which we always seemed to do eventually. Even if England were to win anything in the future, don't get me wrong, I'd love it, but it would never be as good as it would've been in those days. The atmosphere was just brilliant. Oh well. C'est La Vie.

Gigs (Part 3 – Guilfest)

Guilfest was a 3 day festival set in the large fields of Stoke Park, just outside the town of Guildford. What I'm about to write will be comprised of all the times I've been there with different people. It all just kind of blends into one.

I'm not even sure how it all started. I mainly used to go there with Ray (Madness and Pistols) and his good mate Syd who was also a regular from the Hart, and who I mentioned earlier in the book. We all got on really well. We liked to take the piss out of each other (a lot) but you had to be able to receive it too, because it was only a matter of time before it was your turn. On one of the early visits, maybe our second or third time, we found this really nice pub, which was a bit out of the way, but reasonably close to the entrance through a side alleyway. On this occasion, we were all having a great time. The early bands on were a bit

ropey so we spent a long time in there. We eventually

decided that we should probably go to the festival, even

though we were set for the day in the pub. It was a bit silly

really as we missed loads of bands. We did however, learn

from this experience, because the next year, we went to the

same pub, but left after just a round each. Excellent, this

would mean that we would get there nice and early, in

order to catch all of the bands that we wanted to see. Well,

we did - much too early. It was fucking empty!

Syd went off to find the loo as he needed a piss. A good

time to go before they get ruined. I was talking with Ray

for some time when we decided to look for him. Up ahead

there were about 10 individual portaloos. Ray shouted out,

"Syd, where are you?"

We hear from the distance,

"I'm in this one, geez."

Syd calls everyone geez. In fact, for a little while, he worked driving and setting up catering vans for mobile film sets and stuff. On one occasion he found himself on the set to a Cliff Richard video shoot of all things. He actually bumped into Sir Cliff and got chatting. Just when he was about to leave Syd said,

"By the way, what should I call you, Cliff, Sir or Sir Cliff?"

Cliff Richard thought about it and replied,

"Well, what do you call your mates?"

"Well I just call everyone geez" he said.

Now I'm no fan of Cliff Richard, but I thought this was a cool answer. He said,

"Well, you'd better call me geez then!"

Syd smiled and said,

"Ok then geez" and walked off. As he was walking off, Cliff thought better of it and shouted, "Actually, you'd better call me Sir Geez!"

Anyway, the muffled shouting of "I'm in this one geez" was a mistake. A big mistake! Ray ran up to it and started rocking the whole thing backwards and forwards. I wasn't getting involved as I didn't want to get thrown out, before the bloody event even began. There were some good bands playing this year and I didn't want to miss a thing. He's rocking this bloody thing, back and forth. At one point, it seemed to stay on its side for ages as it balanced precariously on the edge of going over completely, but then it rocked back, bang as it hit the ground. I was pissing myself. Ray was loving it. After some loud swearing from inside the portaloo, Syd came out looking like a bloody smurf. He was covered, head to toe in that blue loo stuff or whatever it's called. He stunk of it too. Bleach and piss. To be fair to Syd, he knew what Ray was like and did say,

"It's my own fault. I don't know why I said that I'm in this one."

Most of it did wash off.

I think The Stranglers played that year whose biggest hit was of course Golden Brown. Speaking of which, at one point in the day, we got offered a special, golden brown cake. God knows what was in it but we all tried one.

Myself and Ray went in to the tent to see this band called Drunk In Public, who were an offshoot, acoustic version of The Levellers. Now Ray, I think it's fair to say, has a rather large schnozzle. This special cake was now making us a bit giggly. Also, after consuming the little cake of goodness, Ray's nose was getting even bigger. He looked like Pinocchio without the strings. I couldn't stop laughing and pointing at it. There was a big bloke in front of us shushing me. I hate people talking at gigs so I did get it, but it was all too much. On the 3rd shush, we thought better of it and got out of the tent before we were lynched out of there. A shame as they were really good.

The following year, myself, Ray and Syd were now old hands at this Guilfest thing. The only thing, was picking the best night to go. Friday, Saturday or Sunday. We always seemed to go on the Saturday for convenience, but it was annoying as sometimes Friday would have the better bands. Anyway, this year, the new brigade of Royal Hart goers, the Britpop years if you like, came along as well.

Guilford by train is a bit of a way, and it was sometimes better to change stations somewhere in the middle of Surrey. We'd had a little libation as always. There was this guy Silky. I'd not met him before. I'm not sure if they called him Silky because of his style of playing football, or his way with the ladies. Either way, he was a nice bloke and it suited him. When we changed stations, he was desperate for a piss as were a couple of others. I waited with Ray and the rest of us, two platforms away where our next train was due. Syd was coming out of the loo, not looking like a smurf this time, when he noticed that Silky had gone in one of the traps. Not only this, but for some reason, there was a bolt on the outside of the door. He did what any of us would do – bolt it shut. The train was approaching, Syd and a mad bastard called Brian, were running over laughing as they could hear Silky shouting that he couldn't get out. What happened next was so cool. We all got on the train, laughing at what Syd had done. Silky didn't even have a Guilfest ticket on him, and it was just before mobile phones so he would've been stuck there. He was however, only about 20 and he managed to somehow climb over the cubicle, and was now running over bridge. We'd now been stationary for a couple of minutes. He sprinted to the train and got on just as the doors closed. I thought he'd go mad but he took it well. I thought to myself, he'll fit in.

As I've mentioned before, I really wasn't into drugs at all. I think every drug I've taken (pretty much) has been documented in this bloody book! This time at Guilfest, we were offered some special mushrooms. Well, it's rude to say no. They only became illegal a year later. These were pretty good. I was chatting with Syd and Ray. I suggested to a few people that we should go over to the main stage to see Chumbawamba, but no-one was interested. I was getting a bit mashed up in my head, so I thought I'd have a walk and go and see them. I got knocked down – but I got up again. Sorry, that was lame. Actually, I don't remember much about them at all. I think they were ok. When they came off, I had a walk about to try and clear my head and then went back. I couldn't believe it. They were all where I'd left them. I mentioned that and Syd said something like,

"You've only been gone half an hour."

Now Syd is a piss taking bastard, so I had a go at him for trying to mess with my mind. He wouldn't stop though.

"Span, seriously, you've only been gone half an hour."

I really thought he was messing with me because I'd had these mushrooms. It's the sort of thing he'd do.

Eventually, he said,

"Look at your watch."

I couldn't believe it. It was true. It felt like I'd been gone 2 or 3 hours. That was really weird. With that, the heavens opened and we went into the nearest tent. Not been in here before. It was the comedy tent. There was this bloke on stage. I don't mean to be cruel, but he was fucking shit. There's nothing worse than a really bad comedian. It actually makes you angry! Syd wasn't having any of this. Halfway through the stand up's next 'joke' Syd shouts out,

"Make us laugh."

Everyone looked around at Syd. He got more laughs than the so called comedian who now froze.

"Go on, say something funny!" Syd continued.

Now everyone was laughing at Syd. He could be cruel at times but it was funny. I mean if the comedian was any good, he'd have some kind of retort, but he had nothing in his locker. Nothing. He died a death.

For the rest of the day, I made the mistake of hanging around with Brian. He kept giving me these bloody pills. I mean, if I was sober, I wouldn't have had any of them, but it seemed like a good idea at the time. Later on, when the headline band James came on, everyone was saying that I looked very pale and my lips had turned blue. That was the least of my problems. I felt like Withnail and needed a lie down. It was surreal, as I can remember all this quite clearly. James were playing Laid or something. I love James. Brian and Pipey were properly winding me up saying that I'd shit myself.

"Eughh, look" they kept going.

There were about 6 of us from the Hart all in the same area now. The problem was, those pills were probably laxatives and I really wasn't sure. I remember slyly trying to check. They saw me,

"Eugh, he touched it!" they kept going.

There was nothing there, but those bastards made me believe it for a little while. I still wasn't great but managed to get through the rest of the set and get home and sleep sleep sleep.

Just say no. Seriously.

A few years later, my mates John and Dave and sometimes a few others, would occasionally go. The first year, it was baking hot and everyone got tanned or burnt. We saw The Damned and even had a few words with Dave Vanian later on, as they weren't headlining and he was just milling about. A few more years went by and we decided that we would do the whole festival next year, camping. Myself, John and Dave.

We went up on the Thursday afternoon to try and get a decent pitch. We shouldn't have as 4 nights was way too long. We were miles away from a toilet, so we each had an empty bottle of water to piss in. Very unpleasant after a few days. I think we should've changed bottles! At that time, they were both into smoking weed. That really isn't and never has been my thing, so I left them to it. We hardly saw any bands as they were wasted all the time. We did meet a mate of John's. His name was Womble. What a great nickname. I found out years later that he got it, because he only had one testicle "one ball" - classic!

I was getting a bit fed up. You can only drink so many cans of lager, and they were on a different wavelength. It was pissing down but I didn't care. I went off to see The Icicle Works who I really like. It was now lashing down, and I got totally soaked, head to toe, but I loved it. Nothing makes you feel more alive than being pelted with rain. We even missed Madness on the last night. I mean, we heard them. To be honest, I was knackered by then anyway. We saw a few bands but nowhere near as many as we should've. I reckon we got a maximum of 12 hours sleep over 4 nights. We were knackered come Monday morning. I can't ever remember being that tired, and realised that camping is not for me. I did try it a couple of other times on holiday, but it's not really a holiday, is it?

The following year, I took Lisa and my then young daughter, Amber. I thought it would be a good way for her to experience live music for the first time, as there were kids play areas and stuff. We gave Mark and John a lift up there. Paul Weller and Echo And The Bunneymen were playing that year, but we left midway through Echo And The Bunneymen's set as Amber really had had enough by then, which made it no fun for us. A shame as I'd never seen either of them before.

We had promised to give John and Mark a lift back too unless we got separated. Well, we did and just couldn't find them. I found out later that they were sampling the mushrooms that I'd had the previous year. After a while we gave up and just buggered off. They would have to get a cab back.

Unbeknown to us, they left the park about 2 hours later, right at the end. They managed to somehow find where we parked before, and were sitting on an old Fiat similar to what I had at the time. After about an hour they were wondering where we were. Then Mark realised that it wasn't the same car that they were sitting on. They were laughing but pissed off at the same time, and eventually got a cab back.

My only other memories of Guilfest, were in 2012 when I went with my mate Malcolm to see Gary Numan. I met up with some old Flag mates, Baz and big Steve amongst others. It was a nice sunny day and we were having a laugh. We met up with Gary Numan's wife, Gemma, and a friend of hers. Gemma was saying that Gary was really nervous about doing a festival. I'm not sure that he'd done any before. It must be more anxious knowing that you'll be playing to non fans as well as fans. I reassured her that the vibe was good and there were enough Numan fans there for him to not worry. I don't know if she passed that on to him, but he came out and played a really good set and it went down well.

Over the following few years, the festival really went downhill. They tried to make it too family oriented and got acts in like Olly Murs and The Sugarbabes. Unsurprisingly, that alienated their core audience, the ones who were actually spending money on beer and food. When they made it "family friendly" it would be just that. People would turn up with picnic hampers, the food stalls and beer tents lost money, and it ceased as a music festival a year or two after that. A shame really as we had some really good times there. Nothing beats Syd covered in blue loo though!

Footnote, it seems to have started again under new management but the line ups are still hit and miss.

Hart Transplant To Theatre

The next instalment is pretty vague, although I do remember some bits. I think it was Ray who noticed that there was a play on at the Bush Theatre in Shepherd's Bush. It may have even been me, as I was at the Shepherds Bush Empire quite a bit at the time, which is very nearby. I can't remember the title, but the concept of the play, was that the audience would interact with the players. There was probably no more than 50 or 60 audience members. I don't think we were supposed to interact quite as much as we did, but more on that later. It was one of those coming-of-age type stories, set in the late 70s in the aftermath of punk rock combined with the ska and mod revival. Up the other end of the theatre, there was a stage where some of the actors played a small set of songs. Things like Babylon's Burning and stuff like that.

I have no memory of how we got there, but I know there was a good few of us, maybe about a dozen or so. Just for a change, we had been drinking all day in The Royal Hart on this Saturday. When we got there, I remember Ray saying,

"Act sober" to everyone. "Otherwise, we won't get in."

I think, we just about managed to navigate that first hurdle, and we were in. As I said before, the actors were made out to look like punks, rude boys, rude girls and mods. It was done out quite well, and they made use of the little balconies upstairs, to project their voices from on different levels. I can't really remember the plot that well, but it was the usual story of boy meets girl, girl loves guy, guy is two timing girl, no-one understands me etc etc. We didn't really care about that. We just wanted to be a part of it, and see the band play. It was something a bit different.

It was all going very well. In the play, there was a fight between a mod and his girlfriend at one point. Gay Iain, rather camply and on purpose, began to slap the mod actor on the back of his parka. He was only joking, but you could tell that the actor was getting the hump as he shrugged Iain off. Then, the actress Mina Anwar who has been on TV in things like The Thin Blue Line, Corrie, Shameless and Happy Valley amongst others (thanks Wikipedia!), was doing this monologue in her strong northern accent, dressed in fishnets and punked up gear. It went something like,

"Terry just doesn't understand me, nobody loves me."

For comic effect and because I'd had a load of beer, I blurted out,

"I'll do ya!"

It got a good response from the crowd, but she definitely did me with her off the cuff reply,

"I'm not that fucking desperate!"

I thought it was brilliant. What a great retort. Of course, all my mates were taking the piss and laughing, but I thought it was just as funny as them. Ray's then girlfriend had this

laugh like a donkey. Once she started, that was it. She

started laughing almost as if Eeyore, from Winnie The Poo,

had won the lottery or something. It went on and on. It was

so infectious though. I then couldn't stop laughing. All the

actors were definitely pissed off with us all by now. The

play had come to a standstill, while she tried to stop

guffawing. Deb was stifling her laughter, but I let one more

big laugh out. I couldn't help it. It interrupted their flow

and they stopped. I got daggers from 2 of the actors. I

rather obnoxiously told them to carry on and they did.

What a knob. When they were playing the numbers at the

end of the play, it was great. Like a gig where they played

some of your favourite songs. Iain tried to climb onto the

stage but got shoved off! All a bit embarrassing really, but

overall, apart from the laughing, I think that the actors

actually really enjoyed the improvised spontaneity of it all.

Either that or they thought, what a bunch of dickheads that

lot were, I'm not doing this again!

There Ain't Half Been

Some Clever Bastards

Never a truer word said about Ian Dury. I feel very lucky

and privileged to say that I saw him with The Blockheads

live, many a time from the 90s onwards. It was decided that

a few of us would go and see him at Shepherds Bush

Empire, on 9th December 1995. The Royal Hart had been

put on the backburner for a while, because the current

landlords, Joe and Jo had moved to The Dog And Partridge

over the other side of Ashford. The football team was going

strong now and we had 3 teams in the league. I never

played but I trained a few times. I was always kicking a

ball about as a kid. I was a late developer physically

though, and as a result, I fell out of love with playing the game. When I got into my teens, the sport seemed more about physicality, rather than actual skill. I digress.

Syd's then girlfriend, Linda, said she could give us all a lift to the station in the morning. She ran one of the football teams. There was probably about 6 of us going to this gig. Ray, Syd, Darren, Lee and I think Houndy as well as myself. In the morning, we met up at The Dog, had a couple of beers and set off. We all crammed into the back of her little van.

"What's this?"

We started driving off when I found a bottle of champagne.

"Leave that alone, it's for the league winners" Linda shouted from the front as she was driving.

Someone said that as The Royal Hart were the winners, it must be ours and opened it!

Well, once it was open, it would've been rude not to have any, so we all took turns to have large swigs out of it.

Pretty soon it was empty. Linda was actually ok about it. She knew what we were like. I must admit, by the time we got on the train, I was feeling a little light headed.

We all got to sit together in the carriage, going up to Waterloo which was lucky, because judging by the other passengers, there was a game on at Twickenham. Right behind us were a bunch of big rugby types, and they were being really loud. I don't know how it started but we were discussing the train that we were on. Most of the old carriages had been phased out, and it was unusual to be back on some of the old stock. It was one of the ones where the door windows would slide up and down and each compartment was private. Most trains now had the push button doors and were more open plan. As we were whizzing along, someone was wondering if the door mechanism was computerised for safety like the new ones. I confidently leant over and said,

"Yes, you can't open the door on these as it's going along, look."

As I unlatched the door, it swung open and went "BANG!!!!!" on to the carriage behind us. Those rugby guys went quiet. It must have really shit them up. It shit me up! A train whizzed by in the opposite direction, and then I went to close the door. Ray got hold of me and stopped me in my tracks, pardon the pun.

"You'll get sucked out!" he goes.

I think he had been watching too many James Bond films. The pressure inside a plane at 30,000 feet, is not exactly the same as a train going at about 40mph, although it did seem bloody fast and noisy with the door open. Best not risk it and we waited until we pulled into the next station before closing it. They're bloody dangerous those old trains you know.

As usual, I don't remember much else about that day except Syd at the gig. We all got quite near the front, and Syd wanted Ian to play Plaistow Patricia. As I'm sure a lot of you will remember, the song starts with just Ian shouting out:

"Arseholes, Bastards, Fucking Cunts And Pricks."

Well, Syd soon got us yelling this out from about halfway through the set. After every track you'd hear "Arseholes, Bastards" etc, etc. This went on for a few songs. Then, Ian Dury looked down to his right at us, gave us a wink, smiled, and said in his gruff voice,

"This next one – is for all the Herberts down the front here. Maybe they'll stop giving me grief now. Arseholes, bastards…."

It was brilliant and made our night. What a gentleman he was. Doing research for this book, I actually checked online to get the gig date, and went through a number of his other sets that he'd played at that time. At the other gigs, they didn't play Plaistow Patricia once, so he definitely did it on the night for us. Very cool. Nice one Syd – and Ian.

There was another time that I want to mention, but before that, there was a Blockheads gig that I couldn't go to. I think it was at Brixton Academy. The next time I saw everyone after this gig, they told me what had happened. It was the usual thing, train up to London, a few beers, watch gig, and come back. The weirdest thing happened though and I wished I was there. When they came out of the venue, a limo pulled up. I think it was Ray who went over thinking he was asking for directions. The driver said,

"Are you the party for Staines?"

They all lived in Ashford, which is right next to Staines. It was like a gift from God. Ashford is about 18 miles away, and over an hour's drive. They of course said yes, and jumped in. The driver dropped them all off one by one.

What are the chances? I bet Bobby Davro was pissed off that night as the limo was apparently for a comedian. He's the only one I can think of that might've had a limo waiting for him back then who lived in the area.

This time though, I went with just Ray and Syd. It was Brixton Academy again. I'd only been there a few times before at that point, and didn't really know the area that well. It had a reputation in those days for muggings and even shootings. Normally, you'd get in and get out. Not us though. It was another brilliant gig from Ian and the Blockheads. It was weird though. When we got out at about 11pm, it was like a Saturday afternoon from where we lived. Fruit and veg stalls were all open as were the countless takeaways. What we really fancied though was another couple of beers for the road, but all the pubs were now shutting. We were mooching about looking for somewhere, when this really tall bloke in a top hat came over. I mean, if you are nearly 7 foot tall, you really don't need to wear a top hat as well, that's just taking the piss! Nevertheless, he said that he could get us into this pub that's having a lock in, but we'll have to buy him a beer to get in. It seemed fair enough. On we went to this pub which was run by an old school Irish fella and the place was pretty full with either Irish or West Indian clientele. We got in, bought him and ourselves a pint. The landlord was a miserable bugger and said,

"Now is your last chance to leave, I'm not opening and closing the door again."

That was fine by us, we weren't in a hurry. He drew all the curtains and then went over to the door. He locked it, bolted it, shut another latch followed by another bolt and another bolt followed by another lock at the bottom. It was like the intro scenes from Porridge.

"Norman Stanley Fletcher" etc etc. We weren't going anywhere!

Despite the lack of genial hosting skills from Mr Paddy Mc
Happy, we found the atmosphere really good as I recall.
The Irish and West Indians didn't mix completely, but they
all seemed to get along well enough. It had the funniest
jukebox in there though. It was made up mostly of The
Pogues, The Dubliners etc or Bob Marley And The Wailers
and Peter Tosh etc. You'd be mellowing out to Exodus one
minute and then they'd be up dancing to Sally Maclenane.
Very strange but it was great. I think it was about 3am by
the time we got out. The lock in was still going strong but
we'd had enough. One of the locals wanted out, so we took
our opportunity to do the same. The landlord had now
cheered up funnily enough.

We went out and I couldn't believe it. Places were still
open. If you fancied some carrots and an orange, you could
knock yourself out. We however, were definitely in need of
more sustenance. To our amazement, there were also a

couple of shit in a tray takeaway places still open. Now, this is where it just gets silly.

We were in there looking to see what delights they had on offer. I think I erred on the side of caution and just got some chips. Syd probably did the same, but Ray opted for a sort of curry and rice concoction. The next bit is sad, funny, and ok, a bit wrong but it did happen. I couldn't have made it up.

It was surreal in there. There was a large black lady giving the bloke taking the orders a real hard time. You could kind of expect that at 3:30 in the morning which it now was, but she had the most annoying, squeaky voice. She just would not stop moaning about her lack of chicken wings. We had that going on, I was now pretty pissed but had a hangover coming on at the same time, and then this guy comes over asking for change. I just ignored him. I wasn't in the mood. He could see that he wasn't going to get anywhere with me, so he attempted to try and get some cash out of Syd. When

Syd was pissed you could tell, he would scrunch his nose up without knowing it. Yes, Syd was definitely pissed and was in playful mood.

It didn't help that the guy was whiney and annoying.

"Why should I just give you my hard earned money?"

"Please, please, just give me it." He replied.

"I'm not just going to give you it; you'll have to earn it."

I'm now thinking for fuck's sake Syd, just give him a pound.

"No, no. Just give me it please."

Syd got out a pound from his pocket.

"Thank you, thank you" the guy tried to take it.

"No, I said you are going to have to earn it." Syd carried on. "Heads or tails."

He could be such a wanker. Syd, I hope you are reading this! The guy continued,

"No, I'm not playing, please just give me the pound."

This went on for about 5 minutes. Syd told him that if he didn't guess, then he was putting the pound back into his pocket, and in fact he did just that.

The guy backtracked and said,

"Okay then, heads."

"No, it's too late. I've put it away now." After more pleading, Syd said OK.

"Heads or tails?"

It was tails. Syd put the pound back into his pocket. Meanwhile, Ray who had been laughing was now feeling uncomfortable like myself. We're both feeling sorry for the fella.

"Best of three!" he shouted.

At first Syd wouldn't entertain the idea, but I guess he thought he could have some more amusement at this guy's expense.

"Ok then, best of 3" Syd replied.

"Heads – Er, no, tails."

"No, heads!"

"Are you sure?"

"Yes, heads."

Syd flipped the coin up in the air. It landed - tails.

"Fuck me, you ain't very lucky are ya."

I think even Syd was feeling bad now. I'm not kidding, the guy kept asking, Syd kept playing heads or tails. He lost about 7 times on the spin so to speak. Whether he shouted heads or tails, it was always the opposite. Syd would not give him his bloody pound though. I mean, I know he would've quite happily if he'd won – however, he didn't, and rules were rules. I saw Ray step in and slyly give him a pound behind Syd's back. Some people just don't have any luck. Poor bloke. I mean, to be fair to Syd, he was expecting to lose at some point but he just didn't.

We made our way home via a very dodgy mini cab that cost next to nothing which was as scary as anything. I still wonder how we didn't end up on the news in a fatal car crash. Yes, he was that bad. Thank God for taxi apps these days.

Fame, Fame, Fatal Fame

Due to my job as a courier and a gig goer, I suppose I've met a few famous people over the years. As a courier, I've probably met people who are famous in their field, but I haven't got a clue who they are. I remember once, I was talking to someone who I'd just collected a parcel from. I was chatting away passing the time. They seemed nice enough. As I walked back to the van, a neighbour came up to me and said,

"Do you realise who you were just talking to?"

Apparently, it was some famous classical pianist. I had no idea and cared even less. Yet, if I bump into a pop star, it's a little different. Putney was good for meeting people. I met the Kula Shaker lads in a little studio there. Crispian Mills and the "Kens" who were ok. I met Stereophonics in Kingston in another studio. Kelly Jones shouted over, "Alright drive?" so I had a little chat with them.

I suppose it would've been rude to reply by saying how shit his band were, but they were also nice enough. Who else? Tim Rice. He's a big fella and he has bad taste in jackets. A really weird one was Ronnie Wood. He was living in Kingston, Surrey. I don't think I'm giving anything away there as it's pretty well known, as he has people over like Ronnie O'Sullivan to play snooker and have parties. I went round to his house to pick up a brilliant painting he'd done of his old Faces mate, Rod Stewart. His then wife dealt with stuff like that, but I walked past him as he was doing a proper fry up. So much dyed hair and I've never seen anyone so stick thin. All bones and nose. I nodded and he nodded back, whilst cooking eggs and bacon in a fountain of oil. How is he so thin! It really was a great painting though and I sent it over to Rod in L.A.

I've mentioned meeting Gary Numan earlier. I've since met him quite a few times. More on that later.

The problem is, I forget who I've met. I suppose I should mention the first famous person I met. I was about 8 years old. Myself and my dad went to the Wimpy in Ashford. In walked Bobby Davro. Bloody hell, that's his second mention in this book. He was just about making it in showbusiness but really early on. My dad knew his dad because they both had shops near each other. He came over, said hello and then without much encouragement, started doing impressions to me. To be fair, they were quite good actually. He did Tommy Cooper and asked me if I knew who it was. I replied,

"Frank Spencer?"

Of course, I was messing about. Then he'd do Frank Spencer and I'd say,

"Is it Frankie Howerd?"

This went on for a few impressions before saying to my dad,

"I can tell he's your son!" and buggered off. He was talented but he went down the middle of the road showbiz end of things.

The next one was in the Triumph motorcycle place which was then in Ashford, Middlesex. It was quite fortuitous, because I would normally go in via the warehouse, but it was closed on this occasion. I'm no bike enthusiast, but it had the best smell in that place. Petrol, oil and testosterone! That would be a good album title. They've since moved premises. I went in for a collection and as I wasn't too busy that day, I just waited in the queue behind about 3 other people. The guy in front of me looked familiar. It looked like the back of Jean-Jacques Burnel, the bass player and co singer, songwriter for The Stranglers. I couldn't quite see if it was him until he got served. I thought it might be as he's always had Triumph motorbikes. There are pictures of him from 1977 with Triumph t-shirts on. Sure enough, it was him. The guy serving, told him that he had to check for something in the back. I thought I've got to say something as he was just standing there waiting. He is much taller than I imagined, and his reputation from the old days precedes him. You don't mess with JJ. He's a 7th Dan in karate.

"Hello JJ – brilliant gig last week."

I'd actually seen them a couple of times in the last month, and the London gig was only last week. He smiled and said,

"Were you there?"

"Yeah, I was right at the front" I continued.

He seemed surprised and asked me what I thought of the gig. Luckily, it had been excellent and we had a chat for about 5 minutes. 5 minutes! I didn't even mean that one. Oh, please yourself.

He was great actually. I guess he's like most people. If you're ok with him, then he'll be alright with you. There are loads of stories about what The Stranglers got up to in the old days, like tying a journalist to the top of The Eiffel Tower, but my favourite one is about when The Stranglers and The Clash supported The Ramones in 1976. Paul Simonon, bass player with The Clash, had a nervous tick where he would spit on the ground - almost constantly. When the two bands passed each other on the stage, JJ thought that Paul spat on him and thumped him. Actually, Ive also heard it the other way round but it doesn't really matter. There was a fight after in the car park. Apparently, Dave Greenfield, keyboard player with The Stranglers, had John Lydon up against an ice cream van! I'd loved to have seen that. JJ and Paul had a fight. Paul didn't know about JJ's karate skills until after, but it was never spoken about again. The press took an instant dislike to The Stranglers after that. The next piece, written by JJ, is taken from

Ratter, an online Stranglers blog.

"I was on the Triumph Scrambler, on my way to see my

son Jeremy's band for the first time. He's the drummer and

the band are called Console Wars. I turned left off

Marylebone Road up towards Swiss Cottage. Just as I

turned, another Triumph, this time a black Bonneville,

turned also and we both stopped at the next set of traffic

lights. We both looked at each other's bikes and the rider of

the Bonnie who is not wearing a full face helmet, unlike

myself, said,

"Nice bike mate".

I replied with something like,

"Yours too".

The lights change and we move on. I now think that I know

that face, and by the next set of traffic lights I know who it

is. We stop and I turned to him and said,

"Is your name Paul?"

He says "Yes?" a bit enquiringly.

"Paul Simonon?"

"Yes"

"I'm Jean-Jacques Burnel"

Paul said "I know you!"

"Yes indeed. I'm glad to see you are riding a Triumph"

He said "Yeah but I preferred it when they had kickstarts"

I said "Yes, but they are more reliable now".

We shook hands and then the traffic lights changed and we were off, him towards Primrose Hill and me towards Finsbury Park.

It's taken us 34 years to shake hands."

How brilliant is that? I know it has nothing to do with me, but it's such a great story, I wanted to share it.

One of the nicest famous people I've met is Scott Gorham, the really long haired guitarist out of Thin Lizzy. He was great. I was collecting from his house.

"Come in, do you want a cup of tea or anything?"

I told him that I'm ok thanks, but I did pop in whilst he was getting everything ready. He apologised for not having the paperwork done. If you don't know, he is American but lives over here in London. We were talking about American politics, current affairs and the world in general. I must've spoken to him for about 15 minutes in his front room. He was sending a couple of guitars over to the States. I've learnt over the years that generally speaking, you are better off pretending that you don't know who famous people are. They are more natural that way. When they know that you know who they are, they can play up to it a bit, whether it's intentional or not. When you think what he must've gone through in the 70s, he turned out really grounded. Nice bloke.

I met Ozzy briefly and Sharon pretty much every day for a few years. Before The Osbornes TV show. They are what they are. The TV show is not exaggerated at all. One day Ozzy was having a row with guitarist Geezer Butler about the quad bikes or something. He had a bad accident on one of them a few months later. Sharon was just very professional and I didn't even know she was his wife at the time.

Another encounter was in around 1992, when I was with Lisa and a few of her goth mates that I'd gotten to know pretty well. Actually, we were all a bit gothed up back then.

It was a Sunday afternoon towards the end of August. A nice sunny day. Someone suggested that we drive to Hersham to go strawberry picking. It's only 4 or 5 miles away and we had nothing better to do. We were just passing time in one of the fields when Mark came over.

"I've just met Jimmy Pursey!"

"I was hanging about when this bloke shouted out – why aren't you lot at Reading?"

Mark was just about to tell the bloke to mind his own business or something, when he said

"Oh, are you Jimmy Pursey?"

Sure enough, it was. Mind you, I wish we were at Reading. Doing some research, I found out that we would've been watching Nick Cave supporting Nirvana.

Mark told us that we can go over to his cabin if we want. He was living in this lodge in the middle of the field next to where you pick the strawberries. Some of the group weren't sure. As a bit of a fan of Sham 69, I encouraged us to go over there so we did. We all shook hands. It was quite funny. I think he only wanted us over so that he could nick our fags to make some spliffs. None of the others still smoked. It was just me and I was trying to cut down so I only had Silk Cut.

"For fuck's sake. Is that all you've got?"

His girlfriend who looked like a French model, made us all a cup of tea and Jimmy proceeded to smoke and start chatting. He'd been watching a tv program on Tourette's Syndrome. Something that fascinates me also. It's so sad yet extremely funny at the same time. He was showing us the video that he'd recorded from tv. Jimmy had a good eye, as when this kid was at the dinner table, he spat out some of his food. Right in the background if you looked carefully, you could see the dog catching it and eating it. It was only a small television compared to nowadays, so it was a good spot. He rewound it a good few times. It was funny.

The only other thing I remember talking to him about was a shit Smash Hits review. He remembered it. It was done by a journalist who called themselves, Red Starr. Jimmy was so incensed at the time, that he went round to the offices in Carnaby Street to have it out with him. He said,

"Look at me. I've always been a skinny fucker. What was I gonna do?"

He made a bit of a kerfuffle and they chucked him out. It probably didn't do the band any favours. He's a bit scatty, Jimmy, but I couldn't help but like him.

I met Rob Brydon and Omid Djalili briefly and both seemed nice enough. I met Kirsty MacColl loads of times when she was still living with record producer, Steve Lillywhite in Ealing. She lived quite near Rat Scabies. They were all decent too. I wish I had some scurrilous stories, but most people are ok. It's the ones who are struggling to get somewhere who are normally the arseholes.

There's probably loads more people that I've met who are famous but I can't remember. Does Richard Archer from Hard-Fi count? This is all leading up to the time that I met someone who I never thought I'd meet in a million years. John Lydon.

It all started when myself and two mates from work, got tickets to go and see Hazel O'Connor, perform 2 sets at The Leicester Square Theatre. Formerly the Notre Dame Hall, the well known punk venue. The first set was to be a normal gig comprising mainly newer stuff I believe. Then, there was to be a break and she'd come out and do the whole of the Breaking Glass album with the full band. That's what we really wanted to see.

I'll mention more of my exploits with Dave (especially) and Harry later but it's easier to keep that separate.

We all decided to meet up quite early, as we'd taken the day off work. I think it was a Friday. We ventured into central London and found this nice old pub just outside Covent Garden. We had a few pints and were having a laugh. It's always good drinking in the daytime, especially if you feel that you should be working. I had something on my mind, but waited until we'd had 4 pints before I mentioned it, in the hope that they would be more relaxed and up for it. A couple of weeks previously, I'd had an email from the John Lydon fan page that I subscribed to. He had just brought out these art works which were also books. Each one was individual and very large. They were well out of my price range though at £400 each if memory serves. The mail out said something like, it's the last opportunity to buy one of these books, and you can meet John himself as he's doing a Q and A in wherever it was, London.

As we'd had a few by now, I thought I'd mention it to the others saying that we could meet John Lydon. Dave straight away was well up for it. Harry went with the flow. I remember Dave asking where it was and all I knew was that it was in Covent Garden somewhere, so I rang Lisa who was now at home. I then had to give her my password and read out the email as again, it was before mobiles were smart phones. It was in a place called The Hospital Club.

We were sat there in the pub imagining what questions we would ask him. I said that I'd got a couple that I can't even remember now. Dave, like myself is a big fan of the Brixton Academy Sex Pistols dvd from a few years ago, called "There'll Always Be An England." Especially the extras on the open top bus. If you haven't seen it, it's very funny. Check it out on YouTube. I said to Dave that he could ask him about that.

We only had about an hour to spare, so we went out and started asking people where The Hospital Club was. It took us a while, but it wasn't far and we soon found it. I kind of lead the way, as it was my email and I knew about the book. We went into this plush hotel. It was very extravagant and palatial.

Footnote. Having recently read Dave Stewart's autobiography, I have since learnt that it was a derelict building that he co bought with his investment group. It was originally an 18th century hospital. They'd done a great job in rebuilding it.

We went over to the receptionist and informed her that we were here for the John Lydon Q and A. She asked me for my name which I told her. She then informed me that we weren't on this list of guests. All the guests were supposed to be either fans who bought the book or journos. I told a little white lie. Actually, it was a great big fat black, out and out lie!

"I'm probably not on the list as I only bought the book online yesterday. We've come up all the way from Cornwall to the book launch. How else would I know it was here?"

"You don't sound Cornish" she replied.

"Well, I've only been living down there for about a year. I've still got my London accent." It's amazing how much more confident you get after a few ales. I was actually quite merry, as we downed the four pints of Stella quite quickly.

I could tell that she didn't really believe us, but didn't want the hassle of dealing with 3 half cut idiots, so she politely asked us to sit on the comfy sofa in the foyer, until our party was called out. It was such a big place. There were 3 or 4 conference rooms so I imagine that there were a few different rooms that were being used.

We sat down with some fellow fans trying to act cool and bluff our way in. It was all thick pile carpet, lavish chandeliers and had an air of elegance. An amazing place actually.

It was cool that we'd got this far, but after about 20 minutes, Dave and Harry were getting a bit impatient. We had our drinking heads on now and we hadn't had a beer for about an hour. As I say, they were getting impatient, but I wasn't going to give up now. Another 10 minutes or so went by, and a young guy with a clipboard turned up and announced that the John Lydon party should follow him up the stairs. There were no more than about 20 of us slowly following him. He turned left and checked everyone in to the inner sanctum. One by one they went in smiling. We were about three quarters of the way back and then it was our turn.

"Name?"

"Mike Slifkin plus 2"

This young lad started fumbling through pages on his clipboard.

"You don't appear to be on the list."

I fake angrily replied,

"Not again. We've just had all this downstairs with the receptionist. She told us that she'd put it right."

Meanwhile, there were a few more people who had arrived and they were forming a queue. I could tell that he was getting a bit flustered, so began to sigh impatiently. He didn't really care and was more concerned about getting everyone in before John and his entourage turned up.

"OK, just go in then."

We'd done it. Blagged our way in. As we went through, there were two glamourous looking girls passing us a glass of champagne each, and we found a table where we sat. The mood had changed. We were all buzzing. Then, one of the girls came over and asked us what we'd like to drink on the house. We had 3 pints of cider and then asked for some more. We managed to get another 2 rounds in. When everyone had arrived, we asked if there was any spare champagne. She brought over 3 more glasses. Cheeky buggers we were. I don't know about everyone else, but I was well and truly on the way. Harry had had enough champagne, so myself and Dave had his share as well. We were giggling like little kids now. About another hour had gone by, and it was like we were back in the pub. Suddenly, John Lydon strolls in with a small entourage. The first thing I heard him say was "Someone get me a bottle of lager."

On each table, there was a cardboard advert for the book. I picked one up and we all followed John over to the main area. There was a great vibe. I still remember some of the fans staring at John, not believing they were so close to him. Me included to be honest. If you'd told me, when I was at school in 1978, that I would one day meet Johnny Rotten, I would never have believed it. OK, in some people's minds he has become a bit of a joke, but you can't deny that he almost single-handedly, changed the face of popular culture, and for the better in my opinion. There we were, drinking his beer and following him in to where he was being photographed by the press. I took a few photos with my shitty old camera phone, lined up next to the press with their cameras probably costing thousands of pounds.

After a few minutes of that, he got up and went over to the other area where he would talk a bit about the book and then take any questions.

When it was time to ask questions, everyone was really quiet. Seeing as I was well lubricated, I initiated it by asking him something about the book. I mean that's why he was here. No-one asked anything so I asked a few more generic questions. Then someone else asked a few. By now, Dave had found some inner confidence to ask him something.

"John"

"Yes" he half snarled back.

"Um, Brixton……………………"

"Yes"

"Brixton Academy dvd"

Oh dear, Dave had really fucked up and lost his way. John snarled,

"SPIT IT OUT MAN!" like a psychotic headmaster.

Dave had lost the plot now. Utter silence. I couldn't leave him hanging.

"I think he was trying to ask about the Pistols dvd that you did John."

That was enough to set him off. He went on about it, now giving Dave the odd smile as if to say, you fucked up there didn't you, but it was good fun giving you some shit to make you feel worse. It was great actually. After the questions dried up, someone said we could just go over and have a chat with him.

I waited patiently. Unbeknown to me, as I approached John, Harry took a picture of me talking with him. It looks like he's giving me the hairdryer treatment in the photo, but

I'm thankful to have it. I thanked John for the music or something corny like that. In the room, there were a few blow ups of some old photos taken from the book. Right behind John, there was a picture of him from his Sex Pistols heyday with a bottle of lager in his hand. Here I was, 30 plus years later at the time, talking with him as now he had a bottle of lager in his hand. I said,

"Some things never change, eh?" pointing to the picture.

He smiled and said "It's ok, I have a German wife who keeps me in check. She's wonderful."

I said "Shouldn't that be Wunderbar?"

I know it's a bit of a shit joke, but I guess it showed that I was thinking on my feet and it genuinely made him laugh so I was pleased with that. I didn't spend too much time talking to him as there were people waiting now. We shook hands and I went back to Dave and Harry who were both still buzzing. We all were. I think it's admirable that he looked after Nora in her final years.

The only thing was, we'd missed the Hazel O'Connor gig. Dave said that we still might make the second half if we rush over. We ran the whole way. It wasn't far. We got in just before the second set started. The place is quite small. I've been there since to see Frankie Boyle do a warm up set. We just had time to get a quick round in (like we needed it) and sit down. It's an all seater but we were only a few rows from the front. Hazel worked her way through Breaking Glass brilliantly. We were a very overenthusiastic audience and the cellist kept looking over at us trying not to smile. I think she enjoyed our over excitement.

It rounded off what had been an excellent day. Thanks for the free drinks, John.

I suppose I should finish off this chapter with a few people that I would've liked to have met. Laurel and Hardy, Bob

Mortimer and Rik Mayall have made me laugh more than anyone else. Vic and Ade too for that matter, bit I'll end it with two stories that I remember listening to on the radio first hand from two different people. They left an impression on me and I would also have loved to have met them.

The first was on a local radio station some time ago. A satellite tv engineer phoned up to mention the time he met Michael Caine. I've actually been to his house many a time through work, but never met him. This guy turned up to his house in order to set him up for Sky TV. It was a Friday afternoon, and his last call of the week. He was let in by the hired hand and shown in to the lounge, whereupon he was greeted by Michael Caine himself. They got chatting and realised that they had a few things in common. I think Mr Caine was enjoying the company and offered the installer a beer. He said thankyou but not whilst he was working. At the 3rd time of asking, he said, ok then as it's my last job.

Whether Michael Caine was wanting the company or just being mischievous we'll never know, but he kept asking the guy to set up more TVs, thus creating more work. He told him that he was happy to do the extra work, but he would have to phone his wife to let her know where he was, and that he was going to be late home.

"No problem"

The guy got out his mobile phone and got chatting to her when Michael suddenly grabbed the phone off him and said,

"Listen love, I'm sorry but your husband won't be coming home tonight, he's staying here. He's had a couple of drinks and won't be able to drive back until the morning."

Apparently, Michael Caine would not take no for an answer and they stayed up half the night talking and drinking. He had some coffee and breakfast in the morning and went home. Not a lot of people know that. I already liked Michael Caine but I like him even more now.

The other one I heard, was when this guy rang up to talk about his encounter with Irish comedian, Dave Allen. I never really got Dave Allen when I was a kid, but now I think he was brilliant. Very brave at the time and so subversive. This guy on the radio said how he used to work at the BBC in Wood Lane. He worked with his wife, and on one occasion they got in the lift to leave together. On the way down, the lift stopped and Dave Allen walked in.

"I wonder, could you please tell me where I can find so and so?" he said.

Recognising him straight away, he said, "I'll take you straight there myself Mr Allen." They exchanged names, let's call them John and Irene. It was a bit out of the way and they had a good chat sharing a laugh or two. When they eventually got there, the guy he had a meeting with was angry because he was really late.

"I'm so sorry, I would've got here much earlier but I just couldn't get away from John and Irene!"

As he said this, he gave them a wink and that was that. Quality. You have to learn to think on your feet sometimes.

Holidays In The Sun

When I started writing this book, I had what I thought were so many memories from my days of drinking down The Royal Hart, and although many memories came flooding back, I think the alcohol pickling may have done some long lasting damage! Actually, I don't think that at all really. I was never one to cane it despite what it looks like here. I was just a steady, regular drinker, but I do wish I could remember more. I mean, I thought I could write a whole book on Syd alone. There was the time when he got barred from The District Arms in Ashford, so he took off all his clothes and sat on the bar stool until the police came. Or the time when I was out with Ray and Syd. Big Roy, the 25 stone Elvis guy was driving Ray's rather nice Jag. We'd been to a pub and a club to see a band. We got Roy to drop Syd off at work as he was on an early shift at a courier firm, in the warehouse. It was only a small place. We rolled

up; half pissed. Syd was acting sober as he was starting

work. It must've been about 2am. We parked inside the

actual warehouse. We must've looked like a right bunch.

Big Roy got out first, strolling around, chewing gum like he

owned the place. Then Ray like the 5th member of The

Rolling Stones, me, probably in black with a Cure t-shirt on

or something, and then Syd. There were a couple of lads

getting changed who kept very quiet, heads down. We

looked like a distorted mafia or something. There was a

pool table in their little break room, so we took it over for

about an hour and then just pissed off. It was very surreal.

Why we didn't just drop him off I don't know. I don't think

Syd lasted much longer in that job either.

Or there was the time when myself and Mark were in

Staines with the other Ray. It was a good night, but all of

the the pubs shut. I was ready to go home, so was Mark, but

Ray wasn't having any of it. He took us to the Sad Café as

it was called. Sad was the right word for it. I'm going back about 25 years now. Ray paid a fiver each for us all to get in, as we really weren't bothered. He then paid another fiver each for bottles of bud as they didn't have draught. It was awful in there. I said, I can't stand this and we all left. Ray paid £30 for a warm bottle of bud. Terrible place. Some things you just can't explain. Playing pool with Stuart on a Sunday afternoon. We were both ok at it and I even played in the league for a little while, but we just did the most outrageous flukes, and it always seemed to be on a Sunday. Sunday afternoon sessions were my favourite, because not only were you topping up from the night before, but everyone would be in there due to the licensing hours. Like I say, I wish I could remember more. Maybe if you are an old Royal Hart regular, you could write your own turn of events. I'd love to read another person's perspective. This is why I've opened it up to be more of a memoir, I guess.

Speaking of which, the title of this chapter. I was never that big on sunny holidays. I mean, I'm a former goth (kind of) but when our daughter was a young girl, it seemed the right thing to do, so we would go away when we could afford it. Once every year or two. We did the Disneyland thing a couple of times, Rhodes, Majorca and Portugal. It was in Portugal, somewhere on the Algarve, when we decided to go on a small boat trip. The boat was supposed to anchor near this little lagoon, and you could swim in this stunningly blue water in a cave. It looked magical and we were really looking forward to it. This was the reality. We got onboard this catamaran type vessel. Amber was about 10. These older teenagers all ran on and jumped on to the front shouting and screaming like the selfish pricks that they were, getting the best place. We found a nice little place to sit though and after a few minutes, we were off with the sun beating down on us. It was only when we got out of the harbour, and in to the open sea, that we realised how bad it was. The weather had taken a turn for the worse. There would be these large swells, then woosh we'd drop about 10 feet. The guys working the boat were putting a brave face on it, but you could tell that they weren't happy. It got rougher and rougher and rougher. A few people were asking to turn back but they weren't having it. They didn't want to give out any refunds. We were going to this bloody lagoon whether we liked it or not.

It was now getting a bit scary. The youthful exuberance of the teenagers, had now turned into youthful throwing up over the edge. Excellent. I'm very lucky, I've been on a few dodgy boat trips over the years, and I seem to have good sea legs. I was worried about Amber though. She looked petrified. Lisa, to quote a well-known song, had turned a whiter shade of pale. I took care of Amber whilst Lisa fed the fishes (if you see what I mean) but the best was yet to come. Everyone was in shorts and t-shirts and it was now pretty cold on deck. I managed to get over to the other side where Lisa was chucking up. Amber takes after me re the sea legs thing, so was just about ok, other than being frightened. Lisa still had her head overboard, when one of the ship's crew said he had a cure to stop her from throwing up.

"Yes please" she managed to croak.

With that, he dropped a massive bucket into the ocean, which was connected to a rope, pulled it up and chucked it over her head whilst she wasn't looking. It was like the equivalent of all the water in The Bucket Of Water Song from Tiswas, going over her head in one go. It was so funny. She went mad. The guy said sorry but that it was the only way to stop her throwing up. Fucking brilliant. It did work though!

We had now got to the lagoon, well about 100 yards from it, and it was decided that the waters were too choppy to go any nearer. No shit, Sherlock. We turned back and silently sat on the boat for the return trip for nearly 2 hours. It was very boring and I was also a bit worried about the size of the waves by now. Lisa was shaking with cold. I was still quite amused at seeing her getting soaked, but even that had worn off now. To everyone's relief, we eventually got back to the harbour. Everyone trundled off the catamaran and along the pier to dry land. At the end, there were a couple of the crewmen seeing customers off, looking sheepish as everyone walked off like they had just lost on penalties in the World Cup final. I managed a smile when to my amazement, Amber, who hadn't said a word for the past 3 hours or so,said in an overly posh voice,

"Thank you very much for such an enjoyable trip."

Of course, she was being sarcastic. Some might say taking the piss, but it did make the two guys laugh. I like to think she gets her sense of humour from me and my dad. I know it's their living but they shouldn't have taken us. It was dreadful.

Another eventful trip was before Amber was born, and we went to Paphos in Cyprus. What a great holiday that was. We hope to go back one day, but I've heard that it has changed a lot since we went in the early 90s. Also, in our experience, it never quite works when you do a repeat holiday to the same place.

I remember the first time we went out in the evening. We ordered drinks but when they turned up, they were accompanied by a brandy sour each. I went up to politely explain that we hadn't ordered them. They informed us that they were on the house and it was traditional to serve them up with your first drink. I could get to like this place. We were about a mile or so from the main part of Paphos in a place called Coral Bay. I decided to hire a little moped for the week. It was automatic and although I was drinking, it was kind of the done thing over there at the time. We tried a few different bars but we found one that we particularly liked. They were really friendly, and I'd give the owner the occasional game of pool. It may have changed since then, but the tables had those big balls and pockets. You couldn't bloody miss. After a few evenings going there, he said that his cousin was coming over tomorrow and that he would beat me. I mean, he was slightly better but no chance, and I was only an average pool player. It was all good fun though.

On one occasion, it was only about 9 or 10 in the evening, when I noticed the shutters coming down. It was quiet in there that night, so I said something like, see you tomorrow for our last night.

He said "No, wait 'til everyone has gone. You come with us."

It seemed ominous but we were up for it. Sure enough, everything was locked up and he got in to his Mercedes. Everyone seemed to drive a Merc there. We followed him for a couple of miles when he pulled over.

"We're here!"

I couldn't see what he meant. It was fairly quiet and there was a long old building to the left of us. I must admit, I was a little worried at first. Lisa was giving me one of her looks. He went up to this big oak door and banged on it in code like from an old film or something. Sure enough, the four of them were let in, he said something in Greek, and then he gestured over to us to follow him in. Gulp.

"OK then."

Once we got in, we went down this spiral staircase, and it opened up into what I can only describe as an illegal drinking den. I mean, it may have been legal, but what seemed like all of the Cypriots in Paphos, were drinking and dancing and generally having a good time. I asked them what they wanted to drink.

"No, you're not paying for any drinks tonight. This is on us. Welcome."

It was actually brilliant to think that they were happy to accept us as one of their own. As it happened, we didn't stay that long as we'd already had a few, and I knew I had to drive the two of us back on the coastal road on the moped. I somehow got us back to the hotel unscathed. Such a friendly place though.

Another little break we went on was to Edinburgh. We stayed in this little hotel not far from the castle. A really good location. I have to say, we had a great time. It was rearranged as we had to cancel our first trip due to a family illness. This meant that our original plans to go to a gig, had to go out of the window, so we just went for the hell of it really. We fancied seeing another band though, so I had a scout around, and there was a band on called Duke Spirit. I only knew one of their tracks but I quite liked it.

We quickly checked in to the hotel, and had a look about. I loved all the stone architecture. You appreciate things like that as you get older. We went near the castle but we were visiting that on the next day. Again, it was just before smart phones, and I just could not find this venue. We weren't that bothered, so we looked for a decent pub. We found one and went in, and headed straight for the bar. There was a guy playing guitar and singing along to a drum machine. He was ok. Doing U2, Radiohead. That kind of thing. We decided to stay despite the giant flag above the bar slagging off the English. Not very welcoming. People say that Londoners aren't friendly but you would never get anything like that put up in a London pub. We decided to ignore it. After a couple of drinks, Lisa was befriended by this huge Scottish guy in full kit. Or should that be kilt. We could hardly understand him. Not just his broad accent, but he'd definitely had a few whiskies. We were now about 4 drinks in and he was amusing. It's quite funny. He eventually got

thrown out for some misdemeanour or other. Not to worry.
We were having a good evening. I had a Stranglers t-shirt
on that day and suddenly, three guys came in and
commented on it.

After chatting music to them for a little while, one of them
said,

"Are you going to the gig around the corner?"

"What gig?" was my reply.

"There's some punk bands playing."

I can't remember the name of the venue, but I was up for it.
Lisa wasn't so sure. I had a good chat with one of the lads
who as it turned out was a massive Stranglers and Ramones
fan. Always good chatting about music, and when they
were about to leave, they asked us again. Lisa was well on
the way by now and agreed to come. It really was just
around the corner. We went in and it was brilliant. A tiny
little club full of authentic looking punk rockers. I loved it.

A few bands were playing. It was pretty packed and full of energy. Moshing and stage diving etc. It reminded me of when I first saw Jesus Jones just before they made it. I'd never seen so many stage divers. It was great fun just watching. I love nights out where something unexpected happens. They are usually much better nights than the ones that are organised and carefully planned. We had a great time. I would've stayed until the end but Lisa was knackered by now. I would've said absolutely fucking hanging, but that wouldn't be gentlemanly of me, would it? A great night though.

The next day we looked around the castle. I was very impressed. Built on an extinct volcano fact fans. After that, we went on a tour of the whiskey factory nearby. I'm not that keen on whiskey to be honest. I like a JD but that's different. Mind you, they gave us two shots at the end of the tour. You could really tell the difference between the single malt and the blended. Single malt went down smoothly and blended made you shudder. Still not a fan though really.

These days we tend to do long weekend breaks away with friends. Prague was probably the best. My 50th with old Royal Hart regulars, Steve and Debs was brilliant too. They live in the Dordogne. A beautiful place in the south of France quite near Bergerac. We'd only seen Steve and Debbie once I think in the past 20 odd years since they emigrated. They are the ones who ran Martin's and had the firework party. It was really nice of them to put us up and celebrate my 50th.

It was arranged for Steve to pick us up from the airport. When we met up, it was like we'd only seen him last week. Taking the piss out of each other and just having a laugh. It was about an hour's drive to their place. We got there and I was a little taken aback. I wasn't expecting them to go to any trouble. There were 30 people there including the Mayor all singing Happy Birthday. Ok, I made that last bit up, but they had put Happy 50th banners up, which was really nice of them. Deb had made some homemade hummus which coincidentally, I'd just gotten into. They had a massive outside bar area. I can see why they emigrated there. A really fantastic place. As I recall, we had a few drinks and a look around, but my actual birthday was the next day. We went into town, and noseyed around the market. We bought a massive piece of salmon for that night, as we are technically pescatarians, not vegetarians. Fish and hypocrites, I know. They also drove out and showed us around the countryside. Of course, we popped into a couple of hostelries on the way. Daytime drinking is not good for Lisa. She'd had it by evening with a banging headache. I can't tell you how much we enjoyed our stay. Steve and Debbie were the perfect hosts, and we were reminiscing about the old days. By the time the evening came, we got on it. Well, it was my 50th. Debbie made some amazing cocktails that did the trick. I loved being barman. I'd never been on the other side of the bar before. It was great. They even let me play what music I wanted, which I know is not their taste, but it was brilliant getting slowly sozzled to Ian Dury and the like. I knew I'd had too much to drink when I was dancing. I never dance sober. Debbie decided to bring out the soup she'd prepared earlier. It was quite surreal sipping soup at about 11 in the evening. I was pretty hammered, and Lisa still had a headache, but I had a brilliant time celebrating my 50th. One to remember. Thankyou Steve. Thankyou Debbie. It was brilliant. It would be great to do it again one day. We owe you a meal out. We never did get around to cooking that salmon! That's the thing with the ex Royal Hart lot, you may not see people for years sometimes, but when you do, it's like you haven't been away. The best people.

Gigs (Part 4)

I love going to gigs. I've only scratched the surface of what gigs I've been to over the years. I've never even thought about why I enjoy them so much. I'm not keen on crowds, I don't like drunk people (unless I'm also drunk) and it's sometimes a hassle to get there, and even more so to get back. I guess it started when I was a Gary Numan fan as a kid. My little brain couldn't quite believe that the person I'd idolised on television and in magazines, playing records etc was just over there – like, right now!

Then, each year, following Gary Numan, there would be a new album and tour which were always spectacular and different, right through the eighties actually long after his heyday. Then, over the years, it became quite a social thing as I got to know a few people. I branched out and saw other bands, had a few beers before most shows, and even an average gig was still enjoyable. Some bands have a funny or charismatic front man or woman, others are just powerful live. Some make it seem like an event where we all share this special moment. Mostly though, I just love the music, I guess.

In later years, I started going to see bands again much more often. There were a few of us, instead of going down the pub, which had become a bit boring, we would go and see a band. The internet had arrived and it was much easier to see who was playing, where and when. It was also easier to book tickets online, instead of going to the venue and queueing up at the box office. We started seeing either older bands who we never saw the first time around, or slightly left of centre, up and coming acts. I'd go and see these bands with old mates from The Royal Hart like John, the three Marks, Giggsy, Paul, Dave and a few others as we've now got a WhatsApp group in which we've added more people as the years have gone on. Not forgetting my wife, Lisa who also comes along on occasion. It's great. Most of these gigs were somewhere in London, so we'd get a travelcard and make a day of it, and do a bit of sightseeing via a few pubs of course. We walked almost everywhere, so it was a good way of learning about the geography and history of London too.

Sometimes I'd go and see a band on the spur of the moment with Graham after a home Brentford game too. I was also still on the Numan scene, and the meet ups were now epic as we all knew each other from the various internet forums. There were also a few bands that were connected to the Gary Numan scene in some way. Like myself, longstanding fans mainly. Bands like Tenek, The Thought Criminals, Global Citizen and many more. That is how I got into doing podcasts. More of that later.

I also started seeing bands with a couple of mates at work. Dave and occasionally Harry. It was great because these usually tended to be bigger, more well known acts. Quite naturally, without any planning, I had plenty of gig variety. The weird and wonderful or old punk bands with one group of friends, Numan and connected bands with another, and classic arena bands or bigger bands from whenever, with my work mates. Dexys to Killers. Madness to Oasis and Blur. Occasionally, both lots of groups would combine and meet up which was also really good.

I'll start off with the Numan gigs that were unusual. As stated earlier, I used to mainly go to Hammersmith Odeon every year on my own. Since the Berserker tour in 1984, no-one I knew liked Gary Numan. Well, not enough to go and see him live anyway, especially throughout the eighties. It was at one of these gigs when I met Malcolm. I'd often seen him at Numan concerts, and I went over and started chatting to him as he was also on his own. We got on really well, and it made things easier as we would sometimes get looks as if we were Billy no mates, when we went separately on our own. It was probably in our heads

but then again, we were on our own to be honest. At

Numan gigs anyway. We got to know each other and when

Gary toured, we made arrangements to see him and travel

together quite often. This eventually branched out and I'd

drive us to places like Wolverhampton and Oxford,

normally try and sleep in the car and then drive back. We

had some adventures. I'm sure he won't mind me telling

this. Edit, he suddenly stopped keeping in touch so sod

him! The one that sticks out was when we were in one of

those places. We were drinking very large Jack Daniels and

Coke in the car as a pre gig warm up. I know you're not

supposed to but the car was parked up for the night. It's so

easy to drink when you are in a good mood. We were

chatting about all sorts. After a while and over half a bottle

in, I could tell that he wanted to get something off his chest,

but he kept stopping. I thought he was trying to "come out"

but he just couldn't do it. It had never even crossed my mind before, but I had a hunch so I said,

"If I ask you a question, do you promise that you will answer it honestly?"

He said "Yes."

I said "Are you gay?"

He replied "Yes."

I made it easy for him. Or easier anyway. Of course, he then made it clear that I wasn't his type so no need to worry there. I wasn't worried. I then told him that you must ring Karen. Karen was the girl I went out with years ago, and Malcolm was having an on off relationship with now. Mainly off and she couldn't understand why. She had even phoned me a couple of times to see if I knew why, but I had no answer for her unfortunately.

He phoned her up and I spoke to her first to make it easier for him. He told her what he'd just told me. He came out to two people in one evening for the first time ever. She was relieved, he was relieved and we were both very pissed! That was a good gig.

Whilst Malc was working for British Airways, he managed to get us very cheap flights to see Gary Numan in Manchester. We had such a laugh. I love flying these days and Malc is an aviation enthusiast, so we were both in a good mood. We met at Heathrow, had a couple of beers as usual, and we took off to go to this gig in Manchester. It was so weird, as we landed in less than an hour, and got on a train from Manchester Airport to Piccadilly. The weird thing was, the overground train had those pylons that raise up, and it kind of converts into a tram once you hit the city centre. It was surreal flying, getting on a train, and then stopping right outside the venue. We'd hardly put one foot in front of the other. It was much too early of course, and as we weren't staying anywhere overnight, as we were flying back very early in the morning, have a guess as to what we did? We looked for the nearest decent pub. By the time we got into the venue, we were both pretty far gone. I was worse.

Although I had long given up smoking, we got into the habit of smoking cigars when we went to see Numan. We were quite near the front and waiting for the show to start. For what happened next, I can only apologise. There were two girls in front of us moaning about the cigar smoke. We weren't doing anything wrong, as you were allowed to smoke indoors back then. I hate the smell of smoke now, so I can fully appreciate where they were coming from. Well, after their third dirty look and comment, I'm afraid I flicked some of the cigar ash on their heads. I know (cringe). A few people saw me do it and were actually laughing. That only encouraged me to do it more. Sorry girls, I'm very embarrassed at the thought of it now. I must've been pissed though, because when Gary Numan came on stage, I got on all fours and started crawling through everyone like a lost puppy. I got to the front, turned around and sprang up laughing. To my surprise, everyone was laughing back at what I had done. Very cheeky. I stayed there for the rest of the gig though. I never mean to piss people off, but I do get over excited at times. It was an excellent gig.

We had a chat with a few people that I knew from the forums and in general, trying to extend our evening as long as possible, because the flight back was at about 5 in the morning. We tried to get to the after-show party but failed on this occasion. Then I saw a fairground right outside the venue. We got on this rickety old thing that went miles into the sky. Well, it seemed like it anyway. Then I saw that it had a wheel that you could crank to spin yourself around. I remember yanking it, spinning around and around as fast as I could, whilst we were going up and down and around. Malcolm was pissing himself. Almost literally.

"Stop, or I'll be sick."

Yank, yank, yank. Jesus, now even I was feeling sick. It was a good laugh and a funny way to finish the evening.

We dragged our heels around for as long as we could, and made our way back to the airport where everything had shut down. I was feeling as rough as fuck now. We tried to get our heads down for a few hours in the airport but to no avail. The last thing I remember was flying back to Heathrow. We were still a bit pissed, but hungover at the same time. That seemed to happen a lot. Once we got airborne, they started to bring out the coffee which I was desperate for. Then suddenly, BANG! – we fell from the sky about 20 feet. I just wanted some coffee. This carried on for a little while – please serve me. BANG! – we fell out of the sky again. This was not good for my hangover or my nerves. The in-flight crew weren't happy either so they quickly strapped down the trolleys and themselves. It was awful. Every few minutes, the plane would hit an air pocket. I sniggered to myself as I remembered the story that George told from the old Royal Hart days. Shit, we might be stuck up here for days!

Every now and then there would be another bang, as the hold from underneath, seemed to bang under our seats as we kept hitting turbulence. I've flown a fair bit over the years but nothing has been close to that. Maybe because it was a domestic flight and we didn't go as high up as you do when travelling abroad. Either way, I was actually quite glad that I was tired, hungover and still a little bit pissed, because my senses were not as heightened, and I didn't shit my pants like I'm sure I would've done normally!

On another occasion, a mate of mine, Steve Roper from Norwich had come down with a few others to see Nash The Slash (a Canadian guy who supported Gary on tour a few times) supported by a Numan covers band called Young

Things Don't Scream, a line taken from a Gary Numan song.

I'd already met Steve and the others a few times before, the best time being at Steve's book launch in a pub near Westminster with fellow Nupod dj, Gary Cee. I'm going off on another tangent, aren't I? Oh well, let's go there. It was a great night, meeting up with old friends and talking to some old band members. At the end of the evening, just as we were leaving to head back to the hotel bar, I noticed Steve Webbon demolishing a bottle of red wine. Steve was known to us as being one of the main guys at the Beggars Banquet record company, who dealt Gary Numan back in the day. I thought sod it; I'll say hello.

"Hello, are you Steve Webbon?"

"Do I know you?" he replied.

"Er, no."

"Then fuck off!"

He meant it, but even I had to admit that the comic timing was brilliant. It happened just as Steve Roper walked past, and he pissed himself laughing as I walked away with my tail firmly between my legs. I wish I had a comeback with something highly intellectual and amusing like,

"No, you fuck off." or something, but I just left. To be fair, I'd also had a few by now and didn't have any clue what I was going to say to him anyway. It didn't stop Steve telling everyone and laughing at every given opportunity. Bastard. Mind you, I think I may have done the same if I was in his shoes!

Anyway, some of us met up again to go to this Nash gig in London. Back then, I was not as up to speed with London as much as I am now. We had been in Camden most of the afternoon, as that is where the hotel was. The gig was at the Purple Turtle which I now know as being in Mornington Crescent near Koko, a ten minute walk away. I thought I knew the way, but the walk from Camden seemed longer than I thought. I was getting ribbed at not knowing the way as I was the sole "Londoner". Even though I live about 25 miles away. We beckoned over a black cab and the five of us jumped in.

"Where to?"

"It's not far, The Purple Turtle" I replied. He laughed.

"Are you sure?"

"Yes, we don't know the way."

He must've just got into 3rd gear before he pulled over and we were there. More piss taking from Steve. At least we got there and it was great to see Nash. Sadly, he died only 5 years later. Very sad. Such a talent.

To break it up, I'll save my last Gary Numan gig anecdotes for later on in this long chapter, but next I want to mention the gigs I went to with my work mates Dave and Harry.

It's funny when you meet work mates out of work. Where

we worked, we all had to wear a uniform, so it felt a bit like

seeing your school teacher out of school, wearing casual

clothes or something. I don't know how it started, but Dave

saw loads of bands in the 80s and he always went on his

own. Everyone from Adam & The Ants to Madness and

even Shaky and stuff I would never go to. He's one of

those people who seems to like every kind of music pretty

much. It worked well for about ten years (although

occasionally we still do this) as we would find a band that

we both wanted to see and just book it. Dave, along with

Harry, were the two guys I went with to the John Lydon

book opening. The first gig we went to was when Dexys

Midnight Runners returned to playing live again. It was on

Monday 10th November 2003. We both booked the day off

work and decided to meet up nice and early to have a few

beers. What I hadn't bargained for, was that Dave, although

short in stature, appeared to have hollow legs. I'm a slow

and steady drinker. I like to enjoy a drink and I'll end up a bit pissed but do it in a social way. Not Dave, a pint of stella and I looked around and it had gone. Dave hardly ever drinks at home and can go months without having any alcohol, but when he drinks – he drinks. We found this pub that had a pool table and we settled in there for the afternoon. Me trying to keep up with him. Needless to say, we were both pretty smashed by the time we got to the venue. The Royal Festival Hall near Waterloo. It's more of a theatre than a gig venue and all seated. I met a mate in there and had a chat before the gig. To this day I'm not sure who it was I was talking to. I think it may have been Phil, the old drummer from Kabuki Smiles, but I'm really not sure. The gig was a real disappointment. They came on to one of my favourites, Geno, but it was all slowed down and they were acting out the songs like a 6th form play or something. Terrible. That went into Come On Eileen and they only played another 8 songs after that, and one of them was a cover of The Commodore's hit, Nightshift. Each song was well over 10 minutes long and half the pace. Not my thing at all. At the end, myself and Dave were busting for a piss by now, but it was too much hassle to get up and walk past all the people sitting down. We didn't piss our pants though, we went to the back fire exit and had the best piss ever off the back balcony into the Waterloo air – heaven. Luckily there was nobody below!

Although it was not the best gig, we realised that we got on really well outside of work, and it was still a great day out. With this in mind, we booked loads more gigs. Madness, Tenek, The Sex Pistols, Blancmange, The Boomtown Rats,The Enemy and even Rammstein to name a few. The Damned where I lost my phone because I was pogoing. All sorts and plenty more. Well over 30. We saw The Killers at Earls Court. I liked them at the time although I did go really off them. I actually saw them once before supporting Gary Numan at the Shepherds Bush Empire. I normally didn't bother with support bands, as the meet ups then were excellent due to the increasing popularity of internet forums. Someone had given me a tip off that this band were going to be the next big thing. We got quite near to the front and I enjoyed every second of it. It was just as they were releasing their debut album. I thought they would do well but I could never have predicted that they would do as well as they did. Anyway, like I say, we went to see them a couple of years later and they were now on the stadium circuit. It was an ok gig but we were on the back wall of the balcony. Miles away. I remember looking over at Dave at one point, his eyeballs were swimming around his head. I mentioned that he looked well pissed. He slurred over at me,

"I DON'T FEEL TOO BAD ASHERRRLY!"

I wind him up about that to this day. He says he was putting it on. He wasn't!

One of the best and earliest gigs we went to was Orchestral Manoeuvres In The Dark, doing the whole of their best album in my opinion, Architecture And Morality. This was at my old stomping ground, The Hammersmith Odeon. It was in May 2007. It must have been cold for the time of year as I remember wrapping up in my winter coat, and I decided to bring my headphones to listen to music on the train. Dave wanted to meet up at midday as it was a Saturday. To be fair, I didn't need much persuading. We went from one pub to the next around the Broadwa,y getting more and more sloshed, until the time was ready to go to the venue. When we got there, we were confronted by a small tv crew who wanted to ask us questions. I think this was to go on the dvd extras. That's what they said anyway. The only dvd extras we could've made it on to would've been Rab C Nesbitt's, as we would've been slurring garbled, incoherent nonsense. They said something about meeting us after the show to see what our thoughts were after the gig. We just left.

We had downstairs seats as it was still an all seater venue back then, but our seats were quite near the back. That was no good, I carried on walking past to where there was a group of about 10 empty ones, only about 10 rows from the front. This would do for now at least. We'd move back if we needed to. I joked to Dave that we were lucky that there was a coach crash on the M4 this morning. He started laughing and couldn't stop. You can't beat a bit of dark humour. I was sure that a group would turn up at any minute, but they didn't and we got to stay there. Architecture And Morality is one of the most atmospheric albums I own. I just love it, and to hear it blaring out really loudly was one of those moments. That coupled with an amazing stage set which utilised projection brilliantly, just made it superb. I loved it. After the album was played in full, the band came back for a greatest hits set. A totally different vibe and Andy McCluskey got everyone up dancing. Well, everyone except me of course. The stage was rushed and we found ourselves right at the front now. The gig was being filmed and I was still pissed and on a natural high from the gig, as well as copious amounts of Stella Artois. I was going to do a stage invasion! I tried to clamber up, but I got pushed back. Damn, I wonder if I would've made it on the edit! It was a memorable gig. Up there with one of my favourites.

The only downer was getting home. Dave doesn't live near me, so we said our goodbyes. I got on the train, found a seat, stuck the headphones on, and hunkered down for the journey home in the nice warm train. The next thing I know, I'm being shaken awake by a guard.

"Where are you getting off?"

"Staines" I replied bleary eyed.

"You're here."

In the few seconds that it took for my brain to wake up, I remembered thinking, how does he know that I'm getting off at Staines. Oh well, better get off quick before the train starts again. Well, stumbled on to the platform.

Then reality set in. Hang on a minute. This isn't Staines. I know this place – it's Windsor. The end of the bloody line. Bollocks. I made my way out to see if there was another train going back. There wasn't. Oh no, I don't feel too good. I'm hardly ever sick from drinking, but occasionally it gets the better of me. I met my old adversary, Huey, and tried to sort myself out. It was freezing and I felt like shit. I had £20 left in my pocket and queued for a cab. A people carrier turned up next. I said I'll wait for the next one as there's only me.

"It's OK, where you going?"

"I want to get back to Staines, how much is it?"

He said, it depends on the meter. I said that I had £20 and will that get me there?

He said "Jump in" so I did.

When it got to near where I lived, I cleverly said, anywhere here will do mate. The meter read £26. He pointed to it and said £26. I reminded him that I only had 20 as I said earlier. He started causing a commotion. The more I tried to politely explain the situation, the more obnoxious he got. I was pissed off at him moving the goalposts, so I scrunched up the note and threw it into the front seat and got out. Once I was out of the cab, he waited a bit so I didn't move. He got bored, hooted, and fucked off – so did I, around the corner to where I lived. What a day.

Amongst other bands, Dave was a massive fan of The Specials. By now, we'd been to a fair few gigs and it was a really enjoyable day out. We didn't always get rat arsed but we normally did. This time, Harry was persuaded to come.

The gig was at Brixton Academy but as we had travelcards, I suggested that we go to Camden Town first as it was pretty cool back then, and I'd found out all the decent places to go to have a drink. The idea being that we head over to Brixton later. We went to all the usual haunts that I'd been to with John, and we were having a really good day out. I remember the next bit well. We were in The Elephant's Head. I got an email on my phone from the promoters saying sorry but tonight's gig was cancelled. Terry Hall had lost his voice. Bollocks. I'd never had that happen before. Apart from the Morrissey Madstock incident, but at least the rest of the gig went on that day. I told Harry and Dave that it was cancelled. They didn't believe me of course. Harry did when I showed him the email. Dave still thought I was on a wind up. To be fair, it's the kind of thing I would do. I told him over and over that it was true but the more I said it, the less he believed it. He just laughed or had a blank expression. I told him that it's up to you. They are rescheduling it which was good but it doesn't make it alright. OK, I'll stop now with the bad Specials references. It was only when we got on the tube to go back to Waterloo that he realised. He always lets me do the travel arrangements, so he genuinely thought we were heading towards Brixton, when a group of skins started chatting, saying how gutted they were. Dave's face dropped. He was so pissed off and vowed not to see them again. He did, at least twice. These things occasionally happen.

I'd played Dave some tenek tracks at work and he absolutely loved them. He bought what was available on cd and we pencilled in to see them the next time they played. It was at Electrowerkz, a place I'd been to a few times. As I mentioned earlier, I used to go to The Flag in Wembley regularly. Pete and Frank used to organise it. Sadly, Pete passed away a few years previous, but Frank, to the best of my knowledge still promotes to this day under the name

Flag Promotions. A lot of his events are at Electrowerkz in Angel, Islington. This was one of those events.

We met in Ashford at Harry's house and had a couple of beers. We walked to the station about a mile away. It must have been November time, because we were milling about at the station when suddenly, woooossshhh!!!!!! Fuck me, some bastard aimed a firework at us. It singed a bit of my hair. Could've bloody blinded me. The kids scarpered as soon as we realised what had happened. It got the adrenalin pumping though.

I like Dave and Harry. We wind each other up and take the piss. It's all good, but they - well, Harry especially, is a bit more straight down the line than me. I like things weird and wonderful. I always have. It keeps things entertaining, to a point. Well, this place Electrowerkz is a little unusual. I really like it there. We arrived quite early as the start time was falsely advertised. An old trick to make sure you get people there on time. It's on three floors. The first floor was empty but there was some weird music pumping through the pa. That coupled with loads of dry ice and lasers. It was cool but no-one was in there. Dotted about were a few metal cages, presumably for people to get in to. They were properly freaked out by it. We wandered about and tenek eventually came on really late. I love people watching in places like that.

When we left, we were at the bus stop when another firework whizzed right in between us. How it missed us all I don't know. I ran after the kids this time on the other side of the road, but they got away. I was so angry. Did I have a target on me that day?

Speaking of Flag Promotions, one of the most unusual gigs was when I went to see Adam Ant with Dave and my wife, Lisa. This was when he was trying to make a low key comeback. It was just weird from start to finish. Again, it was in Islington somewhere in a really small club. Another Flag Promotions gig. We got into Islington a couple of hours early for a few drinks. It was up the other end to where I know. We found one pub but after about an hour, we decided to take a walk and find another one, because it was a bit dull in there. We were really looking forward to the gig. Lisa and I had seen him years ago at Shepherds Bush Empire, but we were right at the back and it wasn't with a proper band. Dave had seen him on the Prince Charming Revue back in the day, but that was 30 odd years ago at the time. We walked and walked but there weren't any other pubs nearby. Lisa was getting fed up so we turned around and headed back towards the shit pub. I suggested that we should cross over in case we missed anything, as it was a very wide thoroughfare. It was a warm day and after about ten more minutes of walking, I suddenly saw a pub. I didn't notice it on the other side of the road. We dashed in, and I got us the round that we had all been on. I think I may have been a bit hasty. Just as I'd paid for the drinks, Lisa caught my eye and blurted out

"Err...........naked.........ladies."

Oops, I'd inadvertently taken my wife to a strip joint. I went outside again quickly and this time noticed that the old pub sign had been blacked out. I was so desperate for a drink that I didn't notice.

I said "What do you want to do?"

"Well, we've got our drinks now – let's have these and go."

I'd hoped she would say that. I mean because I was thirsty!

Of course, Dave was pissing himself laughing at me for taking my wife to all the nice places. Most of the time he was just ogling the ladies though. I mean, it was full nudity on display. What Lisa did object to was being asked to pay when one of the strippers kept coming by asking for money. Myself and Dave paid a couple of times and left the dirty mac brigade to it.

It was one to remember though. When we got to the venue, I made a point of asking what time Adam was on, because he was notoriously unconventional at the time. I was

promised that he would be on as advertised which was

about 9pm. There were rumours going around that he was

still in Portsmouth. One support band came on. They

weren't bad. Then another. Then, there was a build up as

the lights went down. Fuck me, it was another support band

and it was now about 9.30pm. I was getting fed up as it was

a week day. We waited a bit longer but now it was 10ish

and Lisa spotted Adam mingling through the crowd. At

least he was here. Another support band came on at 11pm.

He did come on stage and jump about for a bit which was

cool in such a small venue, but it was getting later and later

and we would miss the last train home if we stayed any

longer. I'd had enough. We all had. It's ok if you live in

London but we had to get back. I went downstairs to the

booking office and asked for a refund. £60 for all three

tickets. A bouncer threatened to chuck me out. I told him

that I knew Frank (the promoter) and I wasn't leaving until

I got my money back for all three of us. To be honest, I'd have been happy to get half back as we'd been entertained, but in the end, they gave me a full refund.

We were still pissed off but at least we got our money back. I did some research on the internet the following week. Apparently, he came on stage at midnight, did a blinding set for an hour and a half. Then came back on at 2am and read from Lemmy's autobiography until everyone left! Very Andy Kaufman. I'm glad he's mentally in a better place now. I've seen him a couple of times in recent years doing the really early Antz stuff and it's been brilliant. A true old school showman. It was a weird night though.

As an addendum, myself and Dave also went to an Adam Ant convention prior to this. We knew we were in the right area, but we just couldn't find the venue. It was to be held in a club which was on a high street. I was reading the shop numbers. Only a few had numbers and they were always high up on the signage. As I scanned along, I said to Dave that I think it's over there.

"You think?" he said rather sarcastically.

I didn't know what he meant until my eyes looked down from where I was looking, and there were loads of fans in the Kings Of The Wild Frontier gear and the like queueing up outside. What a numpty, but it was funny. We went in, said hello to a few Numan fans who happened to be there that I knew, but we didn't stay very long. They only had bottled beer and Dave refused to pay £5 a pop. I would've stayed but he was skint. We ended up going back to mine, drinking buds and listened to the first 2 Ants albums. Not quite the same but it was ok.

One of mine and Dave's best days out was when we got tickets to see the Ian Dury biopic, Sex And Drugs And Rock'n'Roll at The Barbican, followed by the German band, Rammstein at Wembley Arena. I met Dave outside the nearest tube station to The Barbican. I'd never been there before and although it was separate from the theatre part, I always wanted to see what it was like inside, so I booked us tickets in advance.

Brutalism architecture is often maligned by the general public, although I think people are coming around to the idea of it nowadays. I wanted to see what it was like for myself. The entrance was near a lit-up tunnel. Very strange and cut off. I'm still not sure if it's for me, but I do like the variety of building styles London has to offer, and taking in London in all its facets, is part of what makes gig going such fun. Just walking the streets. I love it. Normally though, we include a few pubs on our walks, but as we were booked in for the film, I decided to make up a couple of bottles of JD and coke for us. Just to help get us in the mood you understand. It was such a small cinema that we couldn't really drink it in there without disturbing other people, so we watched the film first sans drink. There's nothing worse than idiots making a noise in the cinema, so we didn't want to be those people, unscrewing, swigging, and screwing back up coke bottle tops. The film was really good. We went outside, discussed the film whilst necking the drinks before it became too warm. Maybe a bit too quickly. We were well on the way now and were in pub mode. We'd make our way up to Wembley later on as there aren't many pubs in that area. I don't really like Wembley Arena at all. Not much atmosphere as it's too far away from anything else. It has improved slightly in recent years.

Having said that, we'd had plenty to drink by about 7pm, so we made our way up there in order to try and get near the front. We had standing tickets for downstairs, and I wanted to get close to the front for this gig, as I'd seen some footage of their gigs via a dvd and the internet.

We were well oiled but not too drunk or anything. Dave had been struggling a bit with diarrhoea, which meant I could take the piss out of him for most of the afternoon. It did mean that we got there nice and early though for us, and did get pretty close to the front. Neither of us ever bother drinking whilst the actual gigs were on.

What with the drinking alcohol, diarrhoea and not eating, Dave must have been pretty dehydrated. About half way through the set, and about 3 tons of kerosine used as part of the stage show (Rammstein if you haven't seen them, use a lot of fire in their shows) we were really hot and Dave was definitely bothered. I suddenly noticed that he was gone. I wondered where he was, and thought he must've needed the loo. I was still mesmerised by the show. It really was spectacular. Quite a while later, I saw him running back over and I managed to pull him back in. It turned out, that the St John's Ambulance crew, saw him with his head down not looking very well like he was about to feint. They took him away and he sat down by them whilst they were going to take him out and give him some salts or something. He was already feeling better, and when one of the crew went to sort someone else out who *had* feinted (it was bloody hot in there) he made a dash for it! At least he was back for the encore. I won't go into details what happened next, but we got covered in foam and ticker tape whilst the band were in their final atmospheric crescendo. As a spectacle, it really was up there with one of the best gigs I've seen, and I had the added bonus of taking the piss out of Dave for passing out (nearly) which he still puts down to the diarrhoea. I'm guessing that the booze didn't exactly help either. I've since seen Rammstein again with Lisa outdoors and it was even more spectacular.

It was at the Rocoh Arena, Coventry City's football ground. That was an even more spectacular gig than Wembley. A funny thing happened whilst we were waiting for the show to start. A few guys were chatting behind us in what sounded like Polish. I asked if they could speak English. One of them answered that they can a little. I was only passing time and making small talk. I said,

"I didn't think that Polish and Germans got on very well?"

His answer was brilliant. Without any hesitation he replied,

"It's fine, as long as they are not Nazis!"

What a superb answer. Anyway, back to the other gigs. Hard-fi at Brixton Academy was a good one. They had organised 4 different support acts for the four different sold out shows. This was at the height of their popularity. On the night we went, we saw Billy Bragg supporting. I liked some of his early stuff but would've much preferred Paul Weller who was supporting on another night. Mind you, Richard, the singer and songwriter in the band has since told me, that it was a bit of a pain. Richard wanted Hard-Fi to do Going Underground with Paul, but he wasn't keen. He suggested A Town Called Malice which he still plays and is far more comfortable with. Richard pushed him a bit and they ended up doing both. Paul needed an autocue for his parts though which surprised Richard. I guess he's written a lot of songs over the years.

It was a mad dash to get there as we couldn't get the day off work. It was baking hot, and a long tube journey. We didn't have much time but we were so thirsty. We squeezed into this pub that I knew in Brixton, and ordered 2 bottles of bud each. Both bottles went down in one as we were so parched. That's all we had time for though. We made a mad dash and got there just in time. I like to relax when seeing bands. This was just stressful but it was a great gig. I've seen them a few times before and after, but it was great to see them when they were on top of the world. It seems funny now that I can have a beer and talk to Richard about making cider, discussing music and our beloved Brentford FC. He's a really nice bloke. I think their story is still unfinished. Edit, they have indeed now reformed.

Myself and Graham who I knew from The Royal Hart and Brentford FC, decided to go and see The Good, The Bad, And The Queen at Hammersmith Palais at around this time.

There was talk that we might get back stage after, so Graham said to hang around at the end. I really enjoyed the gig, and I also enjoyed going back to Hammersmith Palais again as it was one of my favourite venues. I'd seen Numan there before and a few others. The first time I went was with some mates from The Hart in 1986. I'm pretty sure Paul and John were there too. It was to see Nina Hagen and Lene Lovich play together. It was a bit too out there even for me. The one thing that did leave an impression on me, not literally unfortunately, was seeing this gorgeous, buxom goth girl walking towards us. She had fishnet stockings over half of her face and over one generously sized breast. Not leaving much to the imagination. Like I say, I love people watching.

Anyway, here we were back again on 31st March 2007. The Good, The Bad And The Queen were a supergroup of sorts. The main songwriter and frontman was Damon Albarn from Blur, you also had Paul Simonon from The Clash, Simon Tong from The Verve and Tony Allen from Fela Kuti. They were touring to promote their debut album which I really liked.

Not only this but one of Britain's greatest living Englishman in my opinion, John Cooper-Clarke was comparing and reciting a few of his iconic poems. I'd always wanted to see JCC live.

He was brilliant of course and did a great job. The Good The Bad And The Queen were also excellent. Damon played a lot of piano and was decked out like a Dickensian urchin. I loved it. After the gig, the lights went up and people were starting to leave. After a few minutes, Paul Simonon came on the stage brandishing an axe. He announced,

"As many of you know, unfortunately The Palais is being knocked down to make flats."

"Lots of boos from everyone."

With reference to the classic Clash single, White Man In Hammersmith Palais, he started chopping up the stage. It wasn't that easy to break. He must've swung at it 10 or 15 times before finally, he got a piece of it up. He held it aloft as if he was the captain of the team at a Wembley Cup Final and proclaimed,

"This is for you Joe."

He left the stage to resounding applause. What Paul Simonon hadn't been told, is that the promoters had now fitted in an extra gig the next evening, which would now be the last one. Ironically, it was The Fall. I hope Mark E Smith didn't 'fall' through the stage!

Just as Graham and I had given up on the idea of getting backstage, (a bit disappointing as at that time, I hadn't met

any of the band) Richard Archer from Hard-fi rang him up.
He said he'd eventually managed to blag a pass for back
stage as all the Hard-fi boys were there. Graham said,

"What about my mate?"

He only had one pass so to cut a long story short, Graham
met Richard who gave Graham the extra pass plus his own,
assuming that he wouldn't need it to get back in. He didn't,
so we were in. Cheers Richard.

We got in and started chatting to the band. They all seemed
decent enough. I then saw John Cooper Clarke on his own
as the person he was talking to had left. I took my
opportunity to go over and say hello. I had a good chat
talking to him. What a top bloke he is.

Then Paul Simonon strolled in looking uber cool in his
natty, trademark pinstriped suit and trilby. There was no
way I was going to get anywhere near him. People were
around him like flies around shit. I was happy though. I've

been backstage at a few places. Shepherd's Bush Empire is a weird one. They have a backstage area which isn't backstage at all. It's high up at the back and there's a pretty big bar. The disappointing thing is that most backstage areas I've been to, you still have to pay for a beer. You do feel privileged though when every so often it happens.

I've just remembered one other thing to do with Richard. As he also lives in Staines, I got to meet him a fair few times and began to know him a little and have the occasional chat. Myself and John had started going to Record Store Days. I'm sure you know this but it's where you can obtain special release vinyl, which is only available for that day. Supposed to be anyway. We decided to get up really early and go to Berwick Street in London's Soho area, as we both wanted a few items. John is more into his reggae box sets amongst other things, and I had my eye on some other releases, mainly the Bladerunner soundtrack on picture disc. We were queueing up for a little while when I noticed someone behind us. I turned around and it was Richard from Hard-Fi. We said hello and got chatting as we'd met him a few time by now. He too was after the Vangelis album. I jokingly said "Wouldn't it be funny if I got the last one."

As fate would have it, that's exactly what happened. You couldn't make it up. I wound him up about that for the next year or two until he did eventually manage to get it online, I'm happy to say.

Dave and Harry had decided to see Oasis at Milton Keynes Bowl. Although I've been to Milton Keynes loads of times to meet up with my old mate Clive, when Brentford used to play MK Dons in the league, however, I'd never been to the Bowl. I wasn't a massive fan of Oasis either. I liked them when they first started, but rapidly went off them.

They persuaded me to go as Harry was driving. I thought it would be a decent day out. The problem was, I'd had a

396

really heavy night down the pub the evening before. Really

heavy. I had a terrible hangover. I thought fuck it; I'll bail

out and stay in to get over my hangover. I was supposed to

meet Dave and Harry in The Moon On The Square in

Feltham. A bit of a dive. They rung my home number. Lisa

came up and gave me earache about letting them down etc.

"OK, tell them I'll get there as soon as I can."

Anything for a quiet life. 2 cups of tea and a bus ride to

Feltham. I went in, the smell of last night's stale lager and

fags made we want to heave. I ordered a large orange juice

with ice. That should help. I was in there for about half an

hour but no sign of them. I was relieved as I thought they

must have gone without me. I phoned Lisa up to see if she

could come and get me as I was still feeling a little fragile.

She said that Dave and Harry were there.

"Oh, for fuck's sake."

They came and picked me up and off we went. Great. I was sat in the back which didn't help how I felt either. Still, my own stupid fault. We eventually got up there, parked in the massive field and walked over to the entrance. Dave and Harry were telling me how they got lost trying to find the car last time that they were both up there. They were well pissed and slept in the car. It was muddy and dark and they fell down a massive bank and knocked themselves out or something stupid. I can't quite remember. At least Harry was not drinking today. Neither was I. I was still feeling pretty ropey. Dave queued up for beer tickets. I hate it when places used to do that. You would have to queue up twice with that system. As the day went on, I felt a little better. We watched The Coral. Very average but kinda ok. I then thought I could manage a drink. I bought 4 tickets as it was cheaper that way and manged to nurse 4 pints slowly throughout the day.

Oasis were also average. No stage presence. They played the tunes just standing there. Dave and Harry seemed to enjoy it a bit more than me. We then made our way back to the car park. We had to queue for another hour just to get out.

One funny thing that happened though, was when we noticed this girl's head bobbing out of the sunroof of a car parked over the other side. Up, down, up, down. It didn't take long for us to realise what was happening. Oh well, another venue ticked off if nothing else.

There's been so many funny incidents with Dave and Harry. Like when we went to see The Boomtown Rats after they reformed in 2013. Wow, only seemed a couple of years ago. The gig was great but I want to mention what happened before we even got to the venue. They always rely on me to get them about, as I know London a bit better and am more organised. I thought I'd teach them a lesson.

We were at our stop on the tube. Normally, I'm up just as the train is about to stop.

Oh, that reminds me. I'm going off tangent again. I was once on my way home from being up London shopping or something. I was on the tube sat opposite this woman. I'm sorry for lowering the tone (a bit late for that I hear you say) but she had the biggest pair of tits you'd ever seen. These things were ridiculous. I was trying as hard as I could, to not look at them seeing as she was sat right opposite. My stop was next and I thought I'd get up out of my seat a bit early. I had a bag in each hand. I don't know why, but the driver put the brakes on quite harshly. I lost my balance and was heading towards her. My hands went out to break the fall, but they were heading for those massive melons. This all happened in a few seconds. I thought I can't break my fall by handling them, so as I got nearer, I pulled them away and held on to the panel behind her. The problem was, my face was now about 2 centimetres from hers. Red faced, I stood up and apologised. She smiled and tried not to laugh as she knew what I'd done. I was trying to be a gentleman.

Back to the journey on the way to the Boomtown Rats gig. I was on the tube train with Dave and Harry, when we were approaching our stop. It was always down to me for organising everything, so like I say, I thought I'd teach them a lesson! I waited until the train was stationary completely, and people were getting off and on. Just as I thought the doors would soon shut, I quickly got up and got off. They both stared at me and started laughing as if I was mucking about. That was until I started laughing back and began to walk down the platform. I had no intention of getting back on to the train. Dave twigged first and quickly got up and ran off just in time. Harry still wasn't sure. Then, he realised that this must be the stop and he decided to get off. The only problem was, he got off just as the doors were shutting. He's quite skinny and the doors shut on his neck. It was so funny. He managed to force the doors back open and jump off. It was a warm day and we were all in t-shirts. Harry's white t-shirt was all scuffed, and he had a thick black line across his neck. I thought it was funny, but Dave was in hysterics. He was laughing flat out through the station like a demented hyena. Harry was pissed off which made it even funnier. Our next train that we had to catch arrived straight away and we jumped on. Dave had tears running down his face. His laughing was infectious and now I couldn't stop laughing. After 2 or 3 more stops, we inadvertently got the whole carriage laughing. After a while, one woman asked what we were laughing at. Dave managed to splutter out what had happened, and started pointing at the mark on Harry's neck. It just made things worse and everyone, I mean everyone in that carriage now started laughing, and were staring at the black line along his neck. Well, one person wasn't laughing. Poor Harry. It was funny though.

There was another time that we all met up. This time we travelled from Harry's place in Ashford. We got the train to Waterloo, and went over the road to The Wellington for a couple of beers. The pub I mentioned much earlier in the book where Buster Edwards used to frequent. They had loads of different bottles of spirits behind the bar. Probably over a hundred. Some of them looked like they hadn't been opened for years. Dave came up with the ingenious idea of choosing one at random, and having it as a shot. I thought it was good for a laugh. Harry thinks of himself as a bit of a connoisseur when it comes to whiskey, which most of the bottles tended to be, and he wanted to choose a specific one. Dave said that that's not the point of it. We just choose one at random, so that's what we did. Dave closed his eyes and pointed.

"Right, we'll have three shots of those please" Dave requested.

It was called Monkey Nuts or something. It had dust on the cap. This was not a good sign. Myself and Dave knocked ours back. God, it was disgusting stuff. Harry the connoisseur was savouring every sip. That was not one of Harry's best decisions. He spent most of the afternoon throwing up. All good ammunition for myself and Dave to take the piss though. This gig was to see Blur in Hyde Park. I saw them in Mile End back in the day. A few of us went from The Royal Hart. It pissed down and I don't remember much about it. The Hyde Park gig was ok but too big for me. I didn't even bother drinking as there was a queue. As you know, I enjoy a drink but as I mentioned earlier, when the band is on, I hardly ever do. I'd rather watch the band. I vowed to never go back to see a gig there again as it's just too big. The amount of people means that tube stations have to close. It's just a hassle. I did go back on my vow though a few years later to see The Who as I'd never seen them. Again, they were ok but it's much too big a venue.

Jonny Marr was probably the highlight for me that day. He was excellent.

The other thing of note with Dave and Harry, was when we left work and met up with some other mates at Shepherd's Bush to see The Stranglers. There's nothing worse than turning up somewhere sober and everyone else is pissed. John and the others got up there late afternoon, so I did my usual trick of making some JD and coke drinks for the journey. I think I did them a bit too strong. When we met up with the others in the pub, they were all pretty sober and we were steaming. Always a good gig though The Stranglers.

I remember seeing them once, it's on Youtube somewhere. Dave Greenfield used to do the keyboard solo to No More Heroes one handed, whilst downing a pint of beer in the other. It would always get a good reaction. This time, after he'd finished, he chucked the empty plastic pint beaker over to JJ, who then kicked it up with his left foot, then passed it over to Baz with his right foot, and Baz headed it into the audience. All whilst they were playing. I don't know if they rehearsed it but it was amazing!

One of the first times that I saw them was on 3rd November 1986 on the Dreamtime Tour. They were supported by Xmal Deutschland and Keith Allen. The unknown Keith Allen was playing a character to wind up the audience. A gay northerner dressed in leather bondage, aiming to get a reaction from the sold out Wembley audience. It worked!

By the time the band came on, Hugh lifted up the biggest bottle of champagne I'd ever seen. It looked like 10 bottles in one. It was a present from the record company. The gig started with Hugh berating the record company, because if they had drunk it, there would've been no gig that night. Then straight into No More Heroes.

Lastly, in 2014 I was double booked. Christmas shopping coincided with myself and Dave having tickets to see

Sparks play, with the 35 piece Heritage Orchestra at The Barbican. Not the cinema this time. In the main concert hall.

Dave decided to join us for the day and we would head off later in the evening, whilst they carried on for the last few hours without us. All was going well. We had a pretty good day out. It was now about 7pm, and myself and Dave headed off to The Barbican. We'd been drinking all day so were well up for it. The first half of the show was to be the whole of 1974's Kimono My House, played with the orchestra to celebrate 40 years since its release. The second half was to be a best of type set.

When we got there, we headed straight to the very posh toilets. It was now about 8pm. Bands don't normally come on until about 8:30 to 9pm. As I came out of the loo, the basins were shared with the ladies for some reason. A rather attractive girl started talking, obviously excited.

"Weren't they great?"

In my head I'm going shit, shit, shit. We must have missed the first set. I couldn't admit to that so I thought on my feet.

"Yeah, can't wait for the second half."

I told Dave what had happened. We checked our tickets. Sure enough, it said program to start at 7pm or something like that. Oh well, at least we had the second half.

We took to our seats in complete silence. This was not right. We'd come from an environment where we were talking and shouting at each other in loud pubs. Now, everyone was sat down in total silence. You could hear the proverbial pin drop, and there was zero atmosphere. A conductor came out, tapped his baton and we were off. It was just not for us. They did Number One Song In Heaven which was brilliant though, plus another couple which were ok. The rest were more of their showtunes type stuff. Myself and Dave were told off for talking a couple of times, and we told them to fuck off. It was shit. Nearly as bad as Dexys. I did get to see Sparks a few years later doing a normal gig at The Forum. That was superb, but I really didn't like the vibe and how poncy the Barbican gig was. A lot of bands are playing classical gigs now, but maybe they are better when there is also a band playing along, like with the Gary Numan and Skaparis Orchestra gigs, although I didn't go to any of those.

Speaking of Gary Numan yet again, I remember him playing at The Marquee in October 1993. He was still doing stuff from Machine And Soul (agreed by most as his worst album) but it was a great setlist. I went with Lisa and some of her mates for a change. There was one thing that was funny. One of the guys who was with us was the spit of Justin Sullivan, the singer in New Model Army. He went up to the bar as it was his round. The girl who was serving mistook him for Justin. He didn't feel the need to put her straight. They got chatting and she went to buy him a drink.

He said that he couldn't accept it as he was getting a round in for his mates.

"Don't worry" she said. This round is on me. We still got him to get the next round in anyway so we all got a free drink!

I should mention when myself and Lisa went on the whole of the Gary Numan UK tour in 1996. He had rediscovered his mojo for the 1994 album, Sacrifice, and I had become a massive fan again. Cars was reissued through being used on Carling Premier's tv ad campaign, and a best of album had done rather well, so a tour was planned in 1996. I really fancied going to as many gigs as I could. I noticed that Pete and Frank were putting on a coach and hotel tour to go alongside for the fans. The hotels were all the same as where Gary and the band were staying, and I thought it would also be a good way of seeing more of the UK. I mentioned it to Lisa that I wanted to go. She's pretty easy going really but said that there was no way that I was going on my own. Fair enough, so we managed to scrape enough money together for us to both go. They weren't cheap hotels, so we could've had a really big holiday abroad for the same price. I don't regret it though; it was great.

We met the coach at Victoria Station in London, and the rest of the itinerary was done for us. I already knew a few of the other fans on the coach at least a little, and I made some good friends in the process during the tour as well. It really felt like we were part of the tour, travelling to and from the various destinations. The problem with organising a tour I guess, is that not all venues are available when you want them. It was 15 dates long, with only one day off. We went from Folkestone eventually up to Glasgow, then slowly back down through Liverpool and eventually back down to Southampton, then back up to Manchester and back down to London travelling nearly 2000 miles! It was great though.

Lisa went to about half of the gigs as she had no need to see him 15 times in 16 days. The first night I thought I'd take in the support band who were called Posh. Not much cop so I didn't bother with support bands after that really. A shame as I missed Mesh a few times, but I did take in the end of Let Loose in Manchester. They were a boy band and the drummer was a big Numan fan, so they got support slot for that one gig. I don't remember it much. Not my thing.

Once we had booked in to the new hotel each day, I would put everything away and have a quick shower. It never took me long to get ready, and I'd always be first at the hotel bar. I was normally joined by a lovely couple, Mike and Angela from Chester. They have been together since 1978, and I got to know them really well.

It was great having a couple of beers, talking Numan, and getting to know people. I can't go through everyone that I met but it was just brilliant.

There was a guy called Steve who followed us and slept most nights in his van. He was great fun. He also liked a drink. It was in Birmingham when we all got invited to this nightclub after the gig, Numan and the crew included. It was ok in there but very dated. I would love it now, but it was too nostalgic playing Visage and stuff from 80/82.

We decided to go back to the hotel bar for a beer. Steve turned up absolutely wrecked. He said he'd had 8 pints of lager and he was being very silly, like you would do after 8 pints. After about an hour, we were joined by Gary Numan and his wife, Gemma. Gary wasn't happy as he has always had a bee in his bonnet about nostalgia, so did a bunk from the club like we did. I think he was pleased that he wasn't the only one, and he enjoyed chatting to us and getting it off his chest. The weird thing was, Steve had the most sober conversation with him acting like he was fine. When Gary and Gemma left, I asked him how he did it. He looked at me, sweating and said something like,

"Thank fuck he's gone!"

He was concentrating so hard to act sober, a bit like when you're 18 and you get home from the pub, and your parents are still up and they want to talk to you. You have to try and not slur. When Gary left, he relaxed and I think it took a lot of concentration. He was done in.

I met up with me old mucker Malc a few times on the tour. That was always weird. Meeting him in the middle of nowhere.

It was a real eye opener actually. In Glasgow they go mental. A great crowd there. In Liverpool, I enjoyed visiting the town centre, and walking past the window where Richard And Judy were presenting their daily live tv show. The only downside was when we were in the bar venue in the evening. It was my round and I was bringing back about 5 drinks on a tray. It was pretty crowded in there. This Scally says,

"Give us your money or I'll stab ya."

He showed me a knife he was carrying. I bluffed my way out of it laughing. I said,

"How am I supposed to do that – I've got my hands full!" and just carried on walking hoping that I wasn't gonna get stabbed in the back. This is not me having a go at Scousers. A similar thing happened to me at a Numan gig at Shepherd's Bush Empire. At the other end of The Green, was a cashpoint machine where there were always homeless people sleeping or begging. I went and got some money out, when one of them told me to give them my money or I'll get stabbed. Again, I just walked away hoping that he wasn't following me. You hope that it's just a threat, but you could get unlucky one day. I just hoped for the best and walked on, on both occasions.

The tour was great though. I had a couple of embarrassing moments. I was checking in to one hotel. I needed the loo and noticed an archway to the right of the main desk. It was a sharp turn and I thought that it might lead the way down some stairs to the toilets. As I went in to the arch, it was a dead end and Gary Numan was just standing there, obviously hiding from the coach load of fans that had just come in. I blurted out something like,

"Shit. Don't worry, I won't say anything" He smiled as I did a swift 180 turn!

Another time was when we were all at breakfast, our table happened to be right next to Gary's. I wouldn't disturb him whilst he was having breakfast, but just as he was about to get up, I got up. I went to let him go, but it looked like he was letting me go, so I started walking. The thing is, he wasn't letting me go and it looked like I deliberately pushed in front of him, stopping him from being able to get up. He lost balance and sat down again! He gave me one of those looks. You know those looks.

I felt terrible for a while but it was a genuine 'after you' type moment.

We had a few good after show parties but to be honest, Gary would never stay long. Gemma always wanted to stay but she ended up leaving early as well.

The last night was at Hammersmith. The setlist didn't change much, but it was excellent. Going from Tubeway Army albums through the classic period, and on to Sacrifice and the excellent new tracks from the soon to be released Exile album. We stayed the last night near Heathrow. Instead of getting back on the coach to Victoria, we said our goodbyes and bailed out and went straight home as it was nearer. I had become such a big fan again. I loved the whole thing of travelling. Ipswich was a shithole mind and we got followed there, but I just loved the whole vibe of being on tour. I do see why Gary loves it. There was a real hole left for the next week or so after the tour. I missed it so much. At least we saw him 3 more times in

August. A warm up gig in Battersea, which was weird as it was the first anniversary of Princess Diana's death, and there was a massive vigil nearby. A bit eery. This gig was followed by two V96 appearances, one in Chelmsford and then I drove up to Warrington the next day with Lisa and Malc. What a nutter. It was a good line up though. Got to see Pulp, Supergrass, Cast and Stereolab amongst others.

The weirdest thing at a gig was probably at Killing Joke. I went with some old Numan mates, Pete and Jill. It was at The Forum. I got separated from them for a while as I headed to the front. It was pretty mental there in the mosh pit. They played this track off the new album called Exorcism. It's pretty relentless. I got so into it, that I had an out of body experience. I was kind of floating above my body, looking down. This had happened once before. I decided to go to a Numan gig with Malcolm in Nottingham. I drove there and back on the same night. On the way back, a similar thing happened where I floated out

of my body above looking down. No drink or drugs taken.
Very strange.

A fairly recent gig at Koko was also quite funny. We were
seeing The Damned again. I was just with John for this one.
We were in our favourite little pub opposite, The Lyttelton
Arms, just people watching. In front of us to our left was ex
England footballer Stuart Pearce with some mates, and to
our right was Marco Pirroni from Adam And The Ants. We
were enjoying a few drinks. People were leaving quite early
for the gig, so after a while, we thought we should too in
case it was an early start. We got over there and The
Damned were already on as it *was* an early start for some
reason. A bit like Sparks, we'd missed a few songs already.
It was packed, so we decided to go up the stairs at the back.
We found some seating which a few people were standing
on. We got up too and could see pretty well from there.

The band went in to a great track called Ignite, and the guy
standing next to John on the seating went mad. He was

jumping up and down, air drumming. He must've been in his late 50s. He forgot himself, lost balance, and went flying off the seat into the people in front knocking them flying like bowling pins. It was so funny. He didn't come back though as I think he was embarrassed, so at least we had more space.

Lastly, in this chapter, I'll bring us up to date in what I do now, gig wise. I still go to see Gary Numan sporadically, but although he's still a great performer, the choice of older material isn't varied enough for me to enjoy it as much. I still go and see gigs with Harry and Dave, but not very often as they prefer to see bands that I'm just not into.

Most of the time, I go with John and a few of our mates. Sometimes Lisa comes too. We see bands like The Witchdoktors, The Members, Spizz, The Zipheads, Urban Voodoo Machine, The Damned. The Ruts. Stuff like that. You always get a good show and it's properly live. Pre lockdown we were seeing a band on average every fortnight or so, either in London or a great new venue in Staines called The Hob. Prices have shot up since the pandemic, so we have to pick and choose a bit more carefully these days.

It was watching one of these bands where it all went a bit pear shaped. Myself and John had a gig booked at a great venue in Brighton called The Prince Albert. I'd seen a few bands there in the past. It's a great little venue near the station. We were booked in to see a band we'd seen many times, Urban Voodoo Machine. They play all kinds of music and are just an excellent live band. There's about ten members including two drummers. Each band member is a real character, and you spend most of the evening watching them do something weird and wonderful.

It was touch and go as to whether I would be able to go, as Lisa's dad was very ill. We'd had a very stressful time of it with some family stuff. I really wanted and needed to go, but only with Lisa's blessing. I probably shouldn't have gone in retrospect, but after some consideration, she gave me the green light. John drove us both there and had booked tickets for both nights. He was staying around his old mate Neil's for the second night. I was getting the train back the next day, and providing everything was still ok with Lisa, I had a ticket to see The Icicle Works in London. I'd already seen them at Guilfest as previously mentioned, and they were excellent. Well, like I say, I was mega stressed with family matters. We booked in to our hotel, and went out to hit the bars of Brighton.

I got the first round. No messing with pints. Double JDs and coke. John reciprocated, and this went on for a little while via a series of pubs. When we met up with Neil, we were well on the way. Soon after, we made our way to the Prince Albert.

We watched, shouted out, carried on drinking beer which as I say, I don't normally do during the set. At the end, the singer who sweats profusely beneath his head scarf, under his hat throughout the gig, mops himself up and looks for a volunteer to drink from it. Disgusting. If he gets no volunteers which he normally doesn't, he just wrings it out in to the audience who all back off. Just as he does it. I managed to push Neil right under the human waterfall of sweat, and he couldn't get out of the way in time.

"You bastard!"

Well, it had to be done. I looked at John and he looked wasted. I probably looked it too. The venue part is upstairs, and we decided to pop downstairs for a bit. Better beer options downstairs or the loo. I can't remember why. As he was walking down the steps, it was really slippery from spilt beer. He went tumbling down in a spiral as the steps bared left. He got up and still holding his glass he exclaimed,

"I didn't spill a drop!" Silly sod.

The rest is very hazy. We were talking to everyone. The band, other punters. Fuck knows what we were talking about. John said that the next day, he walked in for gig number two, and the band and various other people kept coming up to him exclaiming,

"Yaaay, how are ya John!"

He had no idea they even knew his name. Anyway, back to the previous night, we eventually left. We hadn't eaten and we needed sustenance - badly. Right opposite was a kebab van. As I'm a veggie, we both opted for a falafel wrap, with all the trimmings and plenty of chilli sauce. We were so ravenous, we noticed that we were both eating the wrapper too!

I was now absolutely wiped out. "Let's get back to the hotel". It was the Holiday Inn by the seafront. That should be easy to find. We were walking for over half an hour and we were still in the high street. I'd had enough. It was cold and windy and I needed my bed. I saw someone walking

by. I felt like Withnail in that classic film saying,

"Are you the farmer? We've gone on holiday by mistake!"

Instead, I said,

"Excuse me, do you know where the sea is?"

John was pissing himself, but the guy did point me in the

right direction. My walking had almost come to a standstill

now. I was completely fucked.

"Come on Span."

"You go on ahead, I need a rest."

I had now stopped. John shouted something back but I

wasn't in the mood. I was having a rest and that was that.

We were walking in to a head wind on the seafront. My

stamina levels were empty. John shouted again.

"We're here you stupid twat!" or some such witticism was

relayed to me.

I looked up, and sure enough, we were only a few feet away. Ha ha. I would've probably found a bench and crashed out there.

When I stay at a hotel and I know I'm gonna be drinking, I like to have a bottle of water on standby. I didn't have (or didn't make) enough time to get one. I crashed out on to my bed fully clothed, room spinning. Bollocks, I've not had that since I was in my early 20s. When it happens, I know I will be sick. I was, I woke up in the night, tried to hold it in, and I'm sorry for this next bit, but it then had to come out and splattered up the walls. I tried to clean it up a bit but not very well. I even tried again in the morning with a banging headache, but it just wouldn't shift. Bloody chilli sauce! Sorry Holiday Inn. I have not been sick since then and don't think I ever will be again. Not from drink anyway.

The next day I was feeling terrible. How John did a second night I really don't know. We took a walk around the market. John bought a pork pie hat. It was amusing as we tried to do the Stan Laurel thing of blowing into your thumb, whilst the hat rises. Even that didn't cheer me up. I was struggling all day. In the end, I left a bit early, jumped onto the train and just went home and drank water. I didn't go to see The Icicle Works. I was sort of ok the day after that.

I don't know if it's because of that, but since then I don't really enjoy being drunk. I like a few to relax. Sometimes a few more, but I don't get absolutely wankered anymore. I don't miss it either. Mind you. Never say never.

Gary & Diane

Diane is an old school friend of Lisa's. I have known her for as long as I've known Lisa. Gary and Diane have been together for nearly as long us, and we have had many a good night out, including the incident mentioned earlier in the book, when Gary walked into the glass doors.

I won't go through them all here, but one incident springs to mind. It was to be Gary's 50th birthday, so they decided to rent a house in the country for the weekend. A very big house as there were ten of us staying there. It was the second time that they'd done this as it went so well last time for their anniversary. Well, apart from setting off the fire alarm and having to call an ambulance, but that's another story. For once, not me to blame.

This time, Diane had obviously done a lot of planning. We were each given a t-shirt to wear on the next day. Each one had a different silly picture of Gary on it, saying Gary's 50th. When we all went down for breakfast, it made Gary laugh and we were encouraged to wear them for the whole day. In the afternoon, we went for a walk and popped into the local pub. We ordered our drinks and sat outside chatting away. Nothing unusual about that you may think. Well, the next thing that happened was one of those surreal coincidences that sometimes just happen.

A party of funeral goers turned up having just had a service at the local crematorium. They all looked at our t-shirts and were doing a double take. Eventually, one of them went up to one of the girls in our group and said,

"This is a bit weird you all having Gary on your t-shirts. We've just been to a funeral and the guy who we just sent off was also called Gary."

With that, our Gary turned around and came over. On his t-shirt it read in bold letters,

"I AM GARY!"

It could've been a bit awkward but they all saw the funny side of it, and it probably cut the ice for their wake. We didn't stay long after that though. Just too weird.

<u>The Epilogue</u>

If you've got this far, I should say thanks for reading. I feel like I should end on an optimistic note.

I was going to end this book with some of my thoughts on life and all that bollocks. It came out a bit patronising though, so thought I'd give it a swerve. Like most people, I'm a bit of a contradiction. I hate violence but I like watching boxing, I've been a vegetarian for well over 30 years, but I can quite happily kill spiders. I believe in truth though I lie a lot. Oh no, that's Phil Oakey isn't it?

Whilst writing down these memories, many more have sprung to mind, some of which weren't interesting enough for the book, but I enjoyed remembering them all the same. I have to say, it's been a therapeutic process, and to be serious for once, the old adage of wake up and smell the coffee seems appropriate. I mean, to really stop for a moment and take stock. We all live so fast – more now than ever. There is no point in living your life and living in the moment if you don't use your memory and reflect upon it. There is no point if you don't stop, remember, and enjoy those experiences. I'm not trying to be profound. I am a bit of a joker and make light of most things, but what is the point if we don't remember. It means nothing. Whether you decide to write it down, talk to friends about past experiences, or just remember them for yourself. It's a really worthwhile process and I'm glad I did it. If I can, you can. You should have a go.

These days, I play table tennis socially and am in a couple of local leagues. I play for my county and my club at national level for the over 40s.

I am also a big fan of Brentford Football Club. I like to see them as much as I can. It's not just the football. I love meeting up with the lads and having a few beers and talking nonsense.

Of course, I still love gig going.

I've been working as a courier for 34 years. It's not a career. It's a way of paying my bills and enabling me to do the things listed above that I enjoy, and providing for my family. That's not to say that I don't enjoy work. I try to at least, and I exchange a fair bit of banter with everyone there. Especially the moaners. They're more of a challenge but I just love making people laugh. To laugh is healthy. Edit, I have had to start a different job since starting this book so it's a bit different at work these days but I still try and enjoy it.

Lastly, and in some ways, the most rewarding, are my podcasts. I've been doing them when not many people knew what a podcast was. I think it was back in 2008, if not before. I was a member of AFE.Net, a Gary Numan online forum. It was full of some real characters both good and bad. Overall, it was a fun place to be. I think it's still going although it died a death really once Facebook started.

Someone had the idea of starting a set of online Gary Numan based podcasts, which were linked to the site. Gary Cee who has become a good mate over the years, needed time off over Christmas as he was a DJ in real life, and did it for a living. He needed a couple of people to cover for him at this time. Myself, along with a few others had a go. I really enjoyed it and haven't looked back since. I like to think that I've got better over the years, and regularly appear in the worldwide alternative charts. I'm not saying I'm a huge podcast sensation or anything, but I'm doing ok within a limited market. The few people that enjoy it, listen regularly and it's a cool thing.

If you fancy having a listen, the main page where you can find the regular podcasters is at

https://www.facebook.com/groups/nupod/

My own page is   https://podreceiver.podomatic.com/

It's called SPANPOD. It's a play on my nickname as well as standing for Synth, Punk, Alternative and Numan.

It's not all Gary Numan. Far from it. I play up and coming bands, as well as classic artists, as do the other shows. As the name suggests, anything from electronic to indie, 80s alternative, punk and occasionally ska. That kind of thing. I talk and have a bit of fun in between segments of songs and features. It's not for everyone as it focuses on alternative music mainly.

I just want to add my thanks to everyone that I've come into contact with. Gary Cee for inspiring me to write this book, having written 2 biographical books himself. Friends both in the real world and online, whether you were mentioned in here or not. Especially those from the Royal Hart days including Lee Brewer for the book title suggestion. Gary Numan for changing my life for the better. Work colleagues past and present, my daughter Amber, and of course my wife, Lisa. It's been fun and long may it continue.

Lastly, keep well, have a laugh and enjoy yourselves, at the risk of getting another Specials pun in, it's later than you think.

Profits from this book will go to

Battersea Dogs and Cats Home,

Old Windsor.

Printed in Dunstable, United Kingdom